Rosalie,

From my heart to your eyes.

Hind Faulkner

2000

BREAKING NEWS: GOD HAS A PLAN

BREAKING NEWS: GOD HAS A PLAN

An Anchorwoman's Journey Through Faith

By
HARRIS FAULKNER

Leathers Publishing
4500 College Blvd.
Leawood, KS 66211
1 / 888 / 888-7696

ACKNOWLEDGMENTS

Thank you to contributing editors, Rebekah Gallon and Jeffrey Drake. The verbatim of a news story I delivered on the air in "God Sends Us Teachers," Chapter Four, was made "TelePrompTer ready" by staff writer/producers at WDAF-TV. Since it was breaking news, it's difficult to know exactly who would have written that story. However, I would like to acknowledge my appreciation to the following people for giving me great words to say on the air during that time: Jennifer Graves, Beth Hammock and Tim Geraghty. Also, the depositions and court papers included in "In a Stalker's Line of Sight," Chapter One, are all public record and can be obtained by reference numbers and request at the Jackson County Courthouse in Kansas City, Missouri.

Photos courtesy of: James Graham/Black in Government Gala, 1996 (page 70) and many friends who are always on hand with a camera at just the right moment.

Cover Photo: Larry Levenson
Cover Stylists: Clarissa Murphy - Cain and Harriet Gordon

ISBN No. 1-58597-011-5

Library of Congress Catalog Card No. 99-075574

First Edition/Printed in the United States of America

Read Productions, Inc. and
Leathers Publishing at 4500 College Blvd., Leawood, KS 66211

DEDICATION

To my best friends, Bob and Shirley,
who also happen to be my parents.
Thank you for believing in me,
even when I doubted myself.

CONTENTS

Headlines

HUNDREDS OF THOUSANDS of people in Kansas City may recognize my name or my face from the evening news. And watching me co-anchor broadcasts, they may think they know my voice.
But the nature of television news is that the journalists best pre-
serve the integrity and credibility of the broadcasts by showing
objectivity when telling stories. In a way this creates a collective
voice — a voice that is not shaken by emotion or shaped by
anything other than the facts. That perhaps is the ideal anyway.
So people who've seen me have never really heard *my* voice until now. In fact, many may be familiar with some personal details
about my life from reading about them in the newspapers. A front-
page article in the *Kansas City Star* ran Thanksgiving weekend in
1995. The article told readers about a landmark case involving a
local news anchor and a man who had stalked her and threatened her life for months. The case challenged Missouri's anit-stalk-
ing law for the first time in Kansas City. And the subject matter of
the article whetted the taste buds of hungry talk show producers
and Hollywood filmmakers who had learned of the trial after a
national press wire service picked up the story.

Suddenly, I'd gone from being a newscaster to a news maker.
And I had to find a way to deal with the new public pressure for
me to talk about a situation that had ended in the courts, but not
in my heart. Saying no to the talk shows and filmmakers was
easy. My life had been spinning out of control for so long, I wasn't
about to hand over the reins to somebody I didn't know. And
truly, the people I wanted to talk to were others like me, specifi-

cally women who had endured being tormented by a stalker. I reached out to small victims' advocacy groups in Kansas City and cities elsewhere in the nation. That was me crawling back to a steady, safe place. Now I'm walking, telling my story in my own voice in hopes that my experiences may shed some light or hope for anyone who's surviving tough times. When people look at me, they see the face of success and happiness. And beneath it is the soul of someone who knows a harsh reality — bad things happen, and no one is exempt. The lesson for me was that those bad things and the good ones are part of a plan — God's plan.

CHAPTER ONE

In a Stalker's Line of Sight

Guns in my house, never. Growing up, Dad had one. He was in the military, and we lived on Army bases from Germany to New Jersey. He used to say a soldier was trained to be ready for anything. Maybe Dad's duty in Vietnam taught him keeping a loaded gun at home was necessary. But that kind of protection was not for me. That's what makes looking back on the spring of 1993 so difficult for me. I had just been promoted to my dream job — co-anchoring the evening news for the NBC station in Kansas City. But the joy over that was overshadowed by the constant fear of someone watching me, pursuing me. It was a time when I did things that went against the grain of what I believed — just to survive.

FOR THE FIFTH NIGHT in a row it was cradled in my hand, under my pillow. I held it with my index finger just off to the side of the trigger and my thumb resting a couple of inches away on the handle. I had to be careful in my sleep not to move my fingers together, accidentally grazing the trigger.

The truth was, I didn't sleep much anyway. So the chances of me shooting myself were relatively slim. The Smith & Wesson pistol looked small enough for me to fire one-handed, but it had enough kick that I needed to steady it with both hands. My gun was loaded with five hollow-point bullets — a police officer suggested that kind.

"Yeah, if it were me or someone I loved in your situation, I'd keep some heat in the house — with premium rounds, too. And I wouldn't just wound the S.O.B., if you know what I mean," the officer said.

Getting a gun had to be done quietly. I couldn't just walk into any local shop — people might recognize me from the evening news. And I couldn't handle having to answer any questions about why a gun was needed or suffer the wrath of anti-gun viewers. After all, before such desperate times, I had been strongly against having weapons in the home. And I still wanted to be.

"What are you gonna use it for?" Bruce Lindsey asked. He was the co-worker who helped me out with my weapon dilemma.

"Well, just protection. Ya know, I just want to establish —" my voice trailed off. The words flowing from my mouth must have sounded as phony as they were. Bruce, a quick-tongued ex-soldier in his 40s, sold guns as a sideline. He loves to tell stories about his younger days fighting in Vietnam. They made him tough and street smart, he says. Maybe that's why he spotted my trouble, even through the story I was trying to feed him.

"Now, little lady, you can't bullshit the captain of bullshit," he said in his deep, commanding voice. Bruce had been a reporter in Kansas City for years before he gave up the street beat for a desk job in the newsroom.

"You're in some kind of trouble. I can smell it on you. Not to mention those big brown eyes of yours have opened up to about the size of silver dollars in the last five minutes. I'll sell you a gun, if you tell me the real deal."

"I think I have a — stalker."

"Well, you either do or ya don't."

"I do."

"The police know about this? I mean, you must have exhausted some resources to get to the point of buying a gun. That is with you being such a — how do I put it — gun hater, and all," Bruce quipped.

"Yes, I've tried everything. A judge granted me an order of protection to try to keep this guy away, but nothing's worked. The police say their hands are tied because there's no law against stalking in Missouri. There's a bill in the works, but, right now, unless the guy attacks me they can only get him for trespassing, harassment, that sort of thing," I said.

"Is that all the police told you?"

"No, one sergeant said he couldn't tell me what to do, but, well, that's where I got the idea about a gun."

"I see. You set up to learn how to use it?"

"What? It's easy. Just point and pull the trigger, right?"

"Harris, a gun has what we call recoil. That's the power released when you fire. You have to know what that feels like and practice a response. You might get off one shot and get knocked over onto your butt. If you missed and he keeps coming, you may not recover in time to fire again. Then he's gotcha!"

Bruce's words cut fear into my heart. How could I shoot a gun if I couldn't even stand talking about it?

"Never mind, Bruce. This was a bad idea," I said.

"You sure?" Bruce asked.

"Yeah, the police will be there for me. No gun," I said, starting to walk away in shock.

"Wait, just wait a minute. Answer me this." Bruce had been standing behind the newsroom assignment desk, which is raised a couple of feet off the ground. It's accessed by three steps. Bruce walked down the steps to look me in the eye.

"Are you prepared to die?" He was graphic with a real tendency to be over-dramatic.

"No, Bruce," I answered sternly.

"Good. Then you must know the first line of defense is self-defense, whether it's with physical training or a weapon. Don't be intimidated by the process. I would suggest you do both — learn to defend your person and learn to fire a gun. I can recommend some programs designed with women in mind, in the area. But don't let fear keep you from defending yourself. Do you understand?"

Bruce was calm, but firm. After months of being stalked, I had to admit he was the first person to talk with me about how not to be a victim.

He did sell me a gun. My friend, Eric Wright, who was an assistant coach with the University of Missouri football program, invited me down to Columbia. He did target practice on a range there all the time and worked with me for hours on my technique and accuracy. My fitness center offered a six-week course in Tae Kwon Do emphasizing some basic self-defense moves.

At least now, if the stalker attacks me, I thought, I'll be able to fight back. But I prayed it would never come to that.

* * * * *

CASE NO. CR94-4718
in the Circuit Court of Jackson County, MO
at Kansas City, Missouri
FOR THE STATE OF MISSOURI,
ANSWERS AND DEPOSITION OF HARRIS K. FAULKNER,
A WITNESS PRODUCED AT THE INSTANCE OF THE DEFENDANT
TAKEN ... ON THE 1st OF DECEMBER 1994.

Page 3
Q. Could you state your full name please for the record?

A. Harris Kimberley Faulkner.

Q. And where do you live?
A. ___ Ward Parkway.

Q. How long have you been living there?
A. Since August of '93.

Q. Where did you live before that?
A. 412 W. 11th Street, downtown in the Quality Hill area.

Page 5
Q. When did you first meet him?
A. June 26, 1991. I remember that date because he had been hired to come into the newsroom to work as a producer, and we were going to be working on a show together.

Q. Where were you working at that time?
A. Channel 9 in Greenville, North Carolina.

Q. That's how you met was through your work?
A. Yes.

Page 11
Q. Why did you want to end the relationship?
A. I think it was about the time I was job hunting ... I suddenly realized that this was not the right person for me. He was very possessive. He felt very threatened by the fact that I needed to travel. I mean, I needed to travel to find a job.

Q. What would he do?
A. He would check up on me. He would call hotels. He would make sure that I was where I said I was supposed to be. I just thought that was invading and bizarre. He would ask my friends about me.

Q. *Is there anything else you can recall about his behavior?*
A. *He lied a lot, and I could not deal with that. I mean, he would lie to me about what he had for dinner. I didn't know he had a prior arrest record in North Carolina until a probation officer came to our job.*

Q. *So by the time you made your decision to come to Kansas City, your understanding was that it was over with him?*
A. *Yes.*

Q. *When you first moved here and he was still in North Carolina, did you continue to talk to each other and write to each other?*
A. *I think he sent me something once, and we talked on the phone a few times. But not to the extent that we had been talking before. I mean, I was busy ... I didn't have time for it.*

Q. *Do you recall when it was that he contacted you to come to Kansas City?*
A. *I think it was in May or June of '92.*

Page 18
Q. *You said that you continued to see each other as friends, but your relationship had changed, is that right?*
A. *Yes. When he first got here, a lot of the things that I really could not stand, the possessiveness and everything from when we were in North Carolina, had kind of dissipated for a little bit. They quickly came back. ... When that reared its ugly head, I just wanted to cut even the friendship. I mean, I just could not deal with that. "Where have you been?" "Who were you with?" I was being interrogated ... and that's just ridiculous.*

Q. *Did you discuss that with him?*
A. *I told him what about his behavior bothered me, but he always promised to change. Sometimes he really would carry out those promises. I mean, he kind of would back off. He had a nasty habit, though, of standing outside my apartment and question-*

*ing my dates when they left. That was one problem that we had
to get settled, but, you know, I'm somewhat of a bleeding heart.*

*I mean, the minute he regained this possessive nature about
him, I should have just said, "Look, buddy, you're out of there!"
And I think that I'm capable of being a good friend. So I was
patient.*

Q. So at the time you weren't afraid of him or anything like that?
A. No, not at that point.

*Q. Okay, he had moved in across the street from your apartment.
Did you eventually not have any contact?*
*A. We played voice-mail exchange, and we had mutual friends.
So it wasn't like we didn't know what was going on with the
other if we wanted to. I think there was a lot more interest on
his end. I just didn't have time to care, quite frankly.*

Q. How long did that continue?
*A. Actually it continued until the very first time that I became
afraid of him. I had gone to Mexico with a girlfriend in April.*

Q. This is April of '93?
A. '93.

* * * * *

"Man, it's hot out here." Polly wiped the sweat from her fore-head. Polly Taylor was my very close friend. And that's saying a lot because women friends are scarce in my life. I just found that men seemed to understand me better. But Polly was different. In many ways she was my hero. Polly could spend hours putting together an Emmy-award winning piece of video, and then go home and leave her work behind at the office. She was a promotions producer at the station where I worked. Her job was to produce short segments, like commercials to get people to want to watch the news on Channel 4. Her stress level on the job was high, just like that of ours in the newsroom. She shared many of the same deadlines. Yet, Polly didn't let any of it get to her. She was just well-balanced.

"Pass me some more sun block, would ya?" Polly took the bottle from me, pouring out some sun block creme into the palm of one of her hands. "Those two guys at the club were cute last night," she continued.

"Oh, yeah, total babes." I talked into a towel that was covering my face. Lying out in the sun is my passion but my mom has always told me, "Protect the skin that you're in." So I cover my face with a white towel to guard against wrinkles. It's worked so far.

"Boy, this is the life. Hey, I'm gonna flag down that beach waitress. Want anything?" Polly asked.

"Sure, only no more strawberry anything! These people are fruit crazy!"

"Harris, we're at a beach resort. What do you expect them to serve — Peppermint Schnapps!"

Whoever said you can never have too much vacation knows the key to my happiness. That week of April 1993 in Acapulco was one of the happiest times of my life. And it came to an abrupt end.

* * * * *

"Polly, wait before we go down to check out. I just want to use the phone once more to check my voice-mail messages at home." I lifted the receiver and began dialing.

"Yeah, I got mine a little while ago. I'll check the bathroom, balcony, closet shelves … got everything." Her voice was fading in and out as she stuck her head in and around different areas checking for any forgotten items.

"Pol. My G—" I said, trying to stay calm.

"What is it?" she ducked her head out of the closet.

"It's my answering machine. It's full and it's a series of calls from the same person — that guy. You know, the one I worked with in North Carolina."

"Yuck, that's creepy. What's he saying? HARRIS, PRINCESS, I

SIMPLY MUST HAVE YOU," she said in a mocking voice.

"Well, something like that," I answered.

"Oh, Harris, I was just kidding." Polly looked concerned. She came and stood near me as I held the receiver to my ear.

"Tell me exactly what he's saying — how many times did he call?" Polly's eyes widened.

"So far, there have been ten — no, now eleven messages. He's saying he misses me in a way that might lead him to take serious measures to ensure I never leave Kansas City again." I leaned the phone away from my ear.

"Okay, that's enough. Hang up. When you get home, save that answering machine tape. You know, just in case," Polly said in a deliberate tone of voice.

"In case of what?" What she said frightened me. For the first time I tasted the lack of control that was about to become very familiar in my life.

"I don't know what. Just save it." Polly looked worried. I'm sure I did, too. As we lugged our heavy suitcases into the elevator on our way down to the lobby, she began trying to get a handle on the situation.

"Men and women just can't be friends," she said.

"Huh?"

"You said this guy moved to Kansas City and wanted help getting a job in one of the local newsrooms. You've been a good friend to him. Now, this." Polly wiped the sweat from her brow. The temperature inside the elevator must have been above 100 degrees. Just hours earlier we had been enjoying the heat — a reprieve from the Midwest cold. Now, with the tension in the air, the heat had become unbearable.

"All along he's wanted to have a relationship with me. I tried that with him, but I just didn't have any strong feelings for him. I don't want to be controlled."

The elevator seemed to be moving in slow motion, leaving us to talk about this subject much longer than I really wanted to at that point. I just wanted to forget about this guy and move on with my life.

"Controlled — sounds more to me like he's threatening you," Polly said matter-of-factly.

Finally, the elevator doors opened and we pulled the luggage to the front desk to check out of the hotel.

"Just to be on the safe side, I'll change my home phone number when we return. And I'll tell him our friendship is over."

"Good. That oughta be enough to get him to back off," Polly said.

* * * * *

Back in Kansas City, my busy schedule resumed. Returning home from the grocery store one night after work, I parked my car by the back door of my apartment building, in its usual spot. I'd gone shopping late because the store was less crowded and getting in and out was easier. It was around midnight. With just two bulging bags to carry, I made my way to the back door which was always locked. Struggling to hold everything, I stretched my arms around the bags so that my hands met in front. I couldn't see them, but I felt the keys on my key ring until finding the right one.

After unlocking the door, the walk up three floors was tiring. There was no elevator in the beautifully refurbished brownstone. It was in an area called Quality Hill, where the jazz and entertainment stars lived in the 1930s and '40s. From some of the buildings' balconies, there was a great view of downtown Kansas City, Missouri, from the structures to the Missouri River that flows not far away, the nearby freeways and more. My building had no balconies, but the vintage architecture made the units very appealing. There were high ceilings with floor-to-ceiling windows and intriguing floor plans. My unit was on the top floor where each apartment had a staircase leading to a second story loft area with two bedrooms and a bathroom. In the daytime, it was very bright and open. Friends told me my Southwest decor with soft pastel colors gave the place a warm feeling, even when it was snowing outside.

On this spring night, the weather was chilly. As soon as I was through the door and had set the bags on the kitchen counter, I shut a window that was left cracked open a bit. That helped ventilate the apartment, since cooking is a favorite pastime of mine. I figured it was safe to leave it open, because my home was so far off the ground. But when I was home, I usually locked myself in. After putting away the groceries, I left the apartment to go to the mailboxes on the first floor. My box was full — mostly bills. The mailboxes sat about ten feet from the front glass security door. I noticed that door was propped open. I could feel the colder air coming into the entryway. I went down four stairs and reached for the phone book that was keeping the door open. Just then, a face popped up out of nowhere. It was my neighbor.

"Hey, Faulkner woman, how was Mexico?" he asked.

"Richard?"

"Yeah, who'd you think it was, the bogeyman? I just bought a new computer table and I'm bringing it in in pieces," Richard answered, out of breath.

"Need some help?"

"Nah. So how was it?"

"Oh, Acapulco was incredibly beautiful with a great party scene. Polly and I had a blast."

As we talked, Richard made several trips from the sidewalk, through the front door, up the stairs, leaving the furniture boxes in front of the mailboxes.

"My buddy dropped me off with all these boxes while he went to park the car. I didn't want to stray too far from the door, since it was open. Never know who might want to sneak in and rob the place," he smiled. Richard was a recent graduate of law school. Nice guy. His buddy, as he called him, was his part-time live-in lover, Damon. The two of them were always inviting me to plays and to do some of the more eclectic activities around the city. That was cool. They were fun to hang out with.

"Well, look, I'm heading up. Long night at work. Say hello to Damon for me."

"Sure, beautiful." Richard removed the phone book that was propping open the door, and I watched it close — the latch made a loud noise that echoed in the empty entryway. All set, I thought.

* * * * *

Sitting on the edge of my bed, sorting through my mail, I sipped a cup of hot tea. My apartment was quiet. The phone seldom rang since I had the number changed. That was a relief. Too tired to finish reading all of the mail, I put it on the nightstand next to my bed, laid down and quickly fell asleep. After a couple of hours, I awakened to the sound of the air conditioning unit going off. Suddenly, my apartment felt so cold, but the A/C hadn't been on in months. Maybe I accidentally hit the thermostat with one of the grocery bags earlier, I thought. The thermostat control is on the wall right by the door. I didn't have my contact lenses in my eyes, so my vision wasn't the best, but I knew every inch of the apartment, so I'd just quickly go downstairs, flip on the heat and hurry back to bed. No problem, I thought.

When I reached the top of the stairs, even though there were no lights left on downstairs, the bottom of the staircase looked illuminated. As I put my foot on the first step to go down, it made a squeaking noise and the light below went out. My God, someone was in my apartment.

"Hello, who's down there?" I asked nervously. Maybe a maintenance guy was there thinking I wouldn't be home.

"You're from the building?" Maybe I imagined the light going on and off and there was really no one there, I thought. Fat chance. There was only one way out of the apartment — down the stairs. There was no phone to call for help in my bedroom. I had to reach the front door or at least the phone in the kitchen. Then I heard his voice.

"I didn't know you were here. Lucky break."

I turned to run back up the stairs. What happened next was like a scene out of a bad, low-budget slasher movie. Somehow, my footing slipped, sending me tumbling down the stairs, landing right at the stalker's feet, face down.

"You dumb bitch — I gotcha now." He grabbed me by the hair on the back of my head, pulling me into him.

"Let me go!" Tears streamed down my face. We struggled — I

got hold of a small lamp that was on an end table near the stairs. I pushed away from him and hurled the lamp at his head. I missed. He dodged the lamp, but tripped on something. I ran for the door which was partially propped open. My neighbors must have heard me screaming. I couldn't make it to the door.

"Shut up! You'll wake up the entire building — you stupid – "

As he made a run for the door, something spilled out of his shirt pocket — papers of some kind all over the floor. And then I saw them — scissors in one of his hands. He knocked me down on his way out and warned me not to get up.

"I'll be back — you know, so we can spend some quality time together." He was laughing.

He ducked into the hallway and left the building. I was shaking uncontrollably. I closed the door and fumbled with the dead bolt to lock it. I suddenly had so much strength — enough to practically lift the living room sofa — positioning it in front of the door. I kept piling furniture up against it — it was like I couldn't stop. My legs were then suddenly weak. I had to crawl to the phone in the kitchen.

"Miss, you've gotta slow down. I can't understand you. Again, someone broke into your apartment?" the 911 operator said.

"He broke in, but he's gone now." My voice was quivering as I tried to hold back the tears.

"Okay, someone from that address called before. Officers are on their way to you now. Stay on the line until they get there. Are you in a safe place?"

I looked up at the sofa and other furniture pressed against the door. "Yes, but they have to catch him. He said he's coming back."

There was a loud knock at the door.

"Ma'am, are you in there?" a male voice spoke. I listened carefully to make sure it wasn't the voice of the stalker.

"Yes, they're here," I told the operator and hung up the phone. The furniture felt a lot heavier the second time around. I had to remove it to get to the door.

"Are you all right in there?" the officer spoke again.

Finally, the doorway was clear and the door was open. The two police officers, a man and a woman, peered in.

"Stacked the furniture up for protection, huh?" the male officer asked.

"Yes," I said weakly. They entered my apartment and asked me all sorts of questions about what happened.

"Are you going to get him? Arrest him?" I asked.

"We have another patrol car going to his apartment. Apparently, we got more than one call from this building," the male officer responded. "You've got a great set of lungs on ya."

Neighbors in the apartments below and across the hall had heard my screams and the physical struggle with the stalker.

"Is anything missing? Did he steal anything?" the female officer asked.

"No, but he had my vacation photos on him. He dropped them somehow." The photos were all over the living room floor. The female officer picked them up.

"Beautiful beach. Where is this?" she asked.

"Mexico. Acapulco."

"This one's torn — no, it looks cut. Did he have scissors?" The officer was very observant.

"Yes, in one hand. He picked them up as he moved toward the door."

"He must have dropped those, too." The male officer picked up the scissors in the hallway. "Are these yours?" He held up the scissors.

"No, mine have a plastic orange handle," I answered.

"Ah, these are black painted steel. This guy's weird. Maybe he was planning to cut up stuff and came across the photos. Where were they?" The officer wrote in his notebook as we talked.

"Right there on the kitchen counter." The kitchen was adjoining the living room with a serving counter. The pictures had been sitting in a brightly colored Kodak packet on that serving counter.

The male officer seemed to be fitting the story together like he was solving a jigsaw puzzle. "Okay, he comes in with scissors, sees the photos, starts to cut one up and —" He was cut off by the noise on his police radio that was attached to his belt.

"We've got him," a voice said loudly over the radio speaker.

"Well, we can ask him what he was doing here," the male officer said.

"Would you come with us to identify the suspect in custody?" the female officer asked.

"Do I have to go to the police station?"

"No, just come downstairs with us. The other officers should be parked out in front of the building," she said.

The stalker was sitting in the back of a squad car. I had been allowed to stand in the apartment building's entryway and look through the glass security doors into the vehicle parked at the curb. Of course, it was him.

The female officer gave me her card, in case I had any questions about the report. She told me a Jackson County assistant prosecutor would probably file charges in the next few hours and I would be contacted to make a formal statement. She stood at the bottom of the stairs that led back up to my apartment. She waited until I was out of sight.

Once inside, my anger set in. My life had been turned upside down by a man whose only response when questioned by police that night was, "I really got to her this time. She was scared, wasn't she? It was great. Did you see the look on her face?"

The officers said he was actually smiling, proud of himself — bragging about this power to control my world.

"She's my ex-girlfriend, ya know. Mine, all mine," he told them.

* * * * *

DEPOSITION (Continued ...)

Page 25

Mrs. Rieg (Jackson Co. Prosecutor): Just for the record, that is a case the defendant plead guilty to. It was a trespassing case number CR ...

Ms. Shostiak (Public Defender): Yes, okay.

Page 28

The Witness (Harris Faulkner): The thing that they (police) remembered was the fact that he had said he would never leave me alone, and he would always be there.

Q. The officers told you that?
A. Yes.

Q. Okay, what was the next thing that happened?
A. Well, I was having lots of hang-ups on my phone. I don't remember when he went into jail and when he got out ... all of a sudden he just appeared again. And he was told to stay away from me, and I had an order of protection put out on him.

Q. When did you get the order of protection?
A. The original one, I would say right after that incident.

Q. That was April of '93?
A. That would have been April, yeah, April or May of '93, right in there.

Q. You have a (greeting) card here. When did you get this card?
A. That one came, I think, probably around May or June. A lot of stuff happened real close together after he got out (of jail) ... I got tons and tons of mail and tons of hang-ups. He broke back into the (apartment) building thinking that I was home, and he had gotten into the maintenance shed.

* * * * *

"Harris Faulkner, you have a phone call waiting in the newsroom. Harris Faulkner, you have a phone call waiting in the newsroom," the voice said over the public announcement speakers throughout the Channel 4 television station.

At just that moment, I was popping two quarters and a nickel into a vending machine. It was my Twizzlers candy break around

4:30 in the afternoon — about 90 minutes away from my first newscast of the evening. The P.A. system could be heard all over the building. There were even speakers outside, so it was no surprise that everyone I passed on my walk back to my desk, on the second floor, told me there was a call for me.

Although many of us in the newsroom were frustrated about it, the fact was, reaching any of us by phone was all too easy. You could call the TV station, ask for anyone you watched on a newscast, and you were put right through to that person. But then again, most people aren't fleeing a stalker, so maybe phone accessibility isn't that big an issue.

The call had been transferred to my line, which was now ringing.

"Hello, newsroom, this is Harris." I was standing, facing my cubicle. Journalism awards and pictures sat on a shelf at eye level. It gave me great joy to study them whenever I was on the phone.

"Is this Harris Faulkner?"

"Yes, who's this?"

"Ms. Faulkner, this is Shelley over in the management office down at Quality Hill. There's been another break-in. It's that stalker guy again. This is getting —"

I dropped into my desk chair. "Oh, my God, when?" My voice trembled. My co-anchor, Phil Witt, sat close enough to see something was wrong. He mouthed the words, "Is everything all right?"

I didn't respond. He stood up. The woman on the phone continued.

"Our maintenance man, you know him. Well, he discovered the maintenance shed had been pried open. The ring with all the unit keys was gone."

"Did he get into the building — my apartment?"

"No, not this time. Look, I hate to bother you with this at work, but I thought you should know."

"No, it's fine, I want to know," I said.

"Well, there's more," Shelley said.

Phil looked so concerned. I scribbled a few words on a sheet of paper on my desk, letting him know everything was all right

— and that I would explain later. Reading the note over my shoulder, he patted me on the back and tried to force a smile and walked away. Phil had been by my side through so much. It was hard for him not to worry. For some people that might have put a terrible strain on their working relationship, but not with Phil. I always say, "If we hadn't met on the job, God would have brought us together as friends another way."

"Ms. Faulkner, are you still there?

"Yes, you said there's more — what?"

"He was armed, carrying a knife." Shelley paused, taking a deep breath. "The building management is going to press charges, but the one cop today said this guy's getting more dangerous. Ms. Faulkner, are you gonna be okay?"

My voice suddenly became calm. After months of keeping up the appearance of normality and consoling those around me who knew what was happening, it was so easy to slip into that mode. Covering up the truth to protect others was becoming my second job.

"Look, Shelley, I've lived in one of your buildings for more than a year now. And I haven't had trouble until recently. Don't worry, this will pass. And sometimes the police say stuff to get you to take things, you know, more seriously. You're doing the right thing by pressing charges. After all, he did break the law. And you could be helping. Your action may be just the thing to deter him from taking further action." I wondered if she could see through the line of crap I was feeding her. Apparently not.

"Ya think this could be the end of it? I hope so," Shelley said.

"Well, Shelley, thank you for the call. I'd better get back to —" she cut me off. She just couldn't let it go.

"It's so scary that he was headed for your apartment with a knife. I mean, if I didn't know better, if you weren't so calm now, I'd think he was coming to, to kill you. But you've reassured me. Everything will be fine," Shelley finished.

"Take care, Shelley," I said dryly. Phil was back at his desk. I hung up the receiver.

"Who was that?" Phil asked.

"The building manager at my apartment building," I answered.

"What did ya do, lose your keys?"

"No, another incident. He got caught breaking into the building, and I wasn't even home. I spent last night at a girlfriend's house."

"That's odd. As much as this guy follows you around, you'd think he'd know where you were. You sure you got the whole story?" Phil said plainly. He was right. Nearly two decades as a journalist served him well. Something was strange, and he called it right away.

Just then, the phone at my desk rang again.

"Newsroom, this is Harris."

"Ms. Faulkner, this is Detective Chris Atwood. I've been assigned to your case."

"My case?"

"Yes, the guy who's been harassing you. I believe you have called him that before." This detective definitely had my attention.

"Detective Atkins?"

"Atwood. Look, I'd like for you to come down to the station. I have some questions for you, and we should talk about this latest incident. The breaking and entering is serious — but it's his M.O. I'm worried about."

"His motive?"

"Let's talk at my desk. How about tomorrow? What time's good for you?"

"Um, well, in the morning. I work at night. Why do you want to talk to me? I wasn't even home last night."

"Ms. Faulkner —"

"Please, call me Harris."

"Harris, I don't want to frighten you, but this guy's a couple of sandwiches short of a full picnic. He's fixated on you, and after last night I'm not so sure he'll stop there. That security guard — things got physical. Please let's talk in person."

"Okay, tomorrow at ten. Where do I go?"

"The Domestic Violence Unit, 2nd floor."

* * * * *

Police Departments are kind of like hospitals. They have their own smell. In Kansas City, Missouri, the building that houses police headquarters is old — 67 years old, to be exact. The parking was designed for criminal traffic decades ago, and except for the upgrade of adding lots nearby, it's pretty much impossible to avoid a long walk to the front doors. It's always windy among the tall buildings downtown, compared with other parts of the Kansas City metro area. That makes the often-long walk feel even longer.

Finally I reached the entrance steps — 18, and through the doors. Have you ever noticed how people look at you at the police department? Even if you've done nothing wrong, the stares make you feel guilty of something. It's enough to make you shout, "Hey, I'm no loser — just here visiting!"

The elevator doors closed, and the mustiness inside was stifling. The woman in front of me had an unpleasant odor — a mix of cigarettes and cheap, strong perfume. About ten of us were crowded into this moving box.

An elderly man near the back had a high-pitched, happy voice. "Aren't you that lady on the news?"

I smiled. His energy was just enough to break the tension I was feeling. "Yes, I'm on Channel 4."

"Watch ya all the time. Say, you look taller — thinner — prettier than you do on TV. I mean, you look good there, but in person—"

"Well, thank you." I turned toward the back of the elevator and reached back to shake his hand. "Thank you very much for watching, and could you say that part about me looking thin again!" People around us laughed.

As the bell sounded and the doors opened to the second floor, the tension returned. My stomach was in knots. I felt cold and hot, at the same time. There was no way to know what Detective Atwood would ask me, but my intuition told me to prepare for the worst. As I exited, just to the left of the elevator there was a glass door. On the door were the words, "Domestic

Violence, KCPD," in black lettering.

The receptionist sat just inside the glass door. She was tackling several incoming calls and managed to smile at me as I walked in.

"I'm Harris Faulkner, here to see Detective Atwood. We have a ten o'clock appointment."

"Yes. Have a seat. I'll call him and let him know you're here. What did we do to get on the evening news?" the receptionist asked, smiling.

"Oh, no, I'm not here for a story," I responded.

"Oh, good, because my hair and make-up are not what they could be," she quipped.

I was so grateful to have jovial people around to take the edge off my nervous tension. First, the guy in the elevator, now this lady. They were both a blessing to me.

"Ms. Faulkner — Harris, good morning. I'm Detective Atwood. It's wonderful to meet you."

The receptionist was motioning wildly. The phone lines continued ringing and lighting up.

"I think you have a fan who wants to meet you," Atwood said.

"Harris, this is Debbie — Debbie — Harris Faulkner from WDAF Channel —"

"Oh, I know what station she's on. These darn phones." The receptionist was forced to pick up the incoming calls.

We exchanged waves, and the detective guided me back through a long sterile hallway, around a few military-style metal desks, through a maze of cubicles to his office space. His gray cubicle was decorated with family pictures and a few personal touches that at least separated it from the long line of identical work spaces.

"Have a seat." Detective Atwood pulled a chair alongside his desk. He sat in a swivel chair, facing me. He had a pad of paper and a pen, ready to take notes.

Atwood was kind and patient, but persistent in questioning me. He wasn't at all like the ogre I had envisioned from his strong voice over the phone. But one thing was certain — he liked to get right to the point.

"Here are some details you may not know about the break-in the other night. The guy who's stalking you pulled a very large knife out from inside his jacket and threatened the security guard at your apartment building. He told the guard that seeing you was a matter of life or death."

"That's not exactly what the apartment manager told me. She said he had a knife, but she didn't mention the guard was in danger. Is he all right?"

"Yeah, he's fine. I did suggest to the management that having a guard who's not armed patrolling the ground of several buildings at night, in the downtown area, is basically useless," Atwood said.

The detective was flipping the pages in a file that was lying next to his notebook on his desk.

"Ah, here we go. These are the statements from each of the parties involved — the suspect, the guard and some couple on the sidewalk who were walking to their unit and saw a little bit of what happened," Atwood continued.

"There were witnesses?" I asked.

"Yep, this guy's getting bold. It wouldn't surprise me if he didn't try this in the daytime."

"By the way, how is it that a guy who follows me around 24 hours a day, tortures me with phone calls, unwanted gifts, says he can't live without me — how is it that this guy breaks into my building for the second time, but doesn't figure out that I'm not home? Is he stupid? Did he take a vacation and lose track of me?"

"Wait, go back. What was that about he can't live without you?"

"Well, actually what he said was that he'll die if I won't let him into my life," I responded.

"Die — how?"

"I dunno. He said we'll die before we're both 30. Is this important?"

"Harris, I'm putting together a collection of facts which, when it's complete, will do two things. One, we'll have a case history on this guy so maybe we can see him put away for a serious crime. Especially if Missouri gets an anti-stalking law on the books. The other thing is all the info from your case could help me build a profile of a stalker. Comparing the actions and motives of the guy stalking you might help us with other cases we're working on," Atwood said, in his most serious tone yet.

There were other victims like me? And they lived in Kansas City? That thought was haunting.

"The look on your face tells me you thought you were alone in this," Atwood said.

"Are there other women my age? I'm 26."

"Your age, younger — older. You name it. In almost all of the cases, the victims are women. Some know their stalkers — others are random strangers. You probably saw a couple of those victims at the courthouse when you were getting your order of protection papers signed by the judge to keep this guy away," Atwood said.

"The line was long that day, but I figured they were all abused wives or there for their kids — you know, domestic stuff," I said.

"Some were, I'm sure. But we have more than two dozen stalking cases right now. Let's get back to your situation. We seem to be jumping around. We have a lot of ground to cover. This may take more than one meeting," Atwood said.

Detective Atwood said it was essential for me to be able to ask questions. He said understanding more about how the law viewed my situation would help me to feel less like a victim and more in charge of my destiny. For example, during one of our talks, Atwood said the stalker was growing impatient with the network of people around me, such as co-workers, friends and police officers. Atwood said those people were becoming new targets for the stalker. In fact, the night the stalker had broken into my apartment building when I wasn't home was evidence of this. Atwood said the stalker bragged to police about scaring one of what he called "my protectors," namely the building's security guard. Atwood said he purposely broke in when I was away, to send the message that anyone who tried to help me was at his mercy. Atwood said this was a bad sign — a sign that the stalker would not back down, no matter who was near me.

Atwood was likable. And he seemed to have my best interest at heart. One day he asked if I would ever consider moving out of my apartment.

"Move and go where?" I asked.

"There are plenty of places that would be more difficult to tamper with," Atwood responded.

"But he'll just find me again, won't he?"

"Yes, no doubt. Harris, if this guy really wanted you dead, you'd be gone by now. There's no home or police force made to protect you if someone's determined to do you harm. That's reality. My guess is he'll wear you down mentally and physically first. I want to see if this guy can be worn down — exhausted to the point where he sees terrorizing you is not worth the effort," Atwood reasoned.

"So you don't think living in an apartment building with a hundred other people, locks on outer doors and a security guard will exhaust him?"

"Well, they haven't so far." Atwood, as usual, got right to the point. "Think about it anyway. By the way, are you going to be in court when they prosecute him for last week's break-in?" Atwood's tone was suggestive. He encouraged me to learn as much about the legal process as possible. He said I'd need that knowledge when we finally went to court for Kansas City's first stalking trial. He was optimistic that my case would be the first to challenge Missouri's new anti-stalking law. I took his advice, watching the break-in case from a secret room with two-way glass where victims can watch and not be seen.

Meanwhile, Atwood's suggestion about changing residences was out of the question. My home was my last stand against the stalker. It had been weeks since he'd broken in or tried to contact me. Of course, he had been in jail awaiting a court date most of that time, but I was still optimistic that with the management, neighbors — everyone looking out — he'd stay away.

* * * * *

DEPOSITION (Continued ...)

Page 32

Mrs. Rieg (Jackson Co. Prosecutor): Yes, just for the record, the defendant did plead guilty (to breaking and entering the apartment building). That's case number 93.

Ms. Shostiak (Public Defender): So you weren't there when any of that occurred?

Witness (Harris Faulkner): No, I didn't see him personally. Around that same time, my car, I had just gotten a Miata. In one of the answering machine messages that he left, he said that car— I really don't want to say this. He said that he thought I liked white men, and that that car was going to attract a lot of—

Witness: Do I have to say this?
Mrs. Rieg: Yes.

Witness: — white dicks and that I should stop driving it. I went out to get in my car one day shortly after that phone message and my car wouldn't start and I had an event to get to right away. It was the Mini Grand Prix in June of '93 charity race that I needed to get to because I was racing in it. I ended up calling a cab to get there because I couldn't deal with the car right then. After the race, I called the dealership. I was really mad because I had just bought this car and now it wasn't running. The manager of the dealership and a mechanic and my closest friend, Ed, and I all showed up at the car that Saturday afternoon, and they lifted the hood and the whole thing was taken apart. We called the police, and they came out and lifted a fingerprint, but the print was smudged. There was a print on the console inside the car. The car window had been — it's soft top. It had been pressed down to get in to pop the hood. The brakes were disconnected. I mean the car was in pieces. We never did get it put back together to where the interior lights would ever come back on. They tried, but they couldn't.

Q. *You never saw anybody out at the car doing anything to the car?*

A. *No, but there was only one person who hated that car.*

Q. *You said that message was on your answering machine?*

A. *My home machine. I changed my number after that. I have changed my number so many times. It doesn't matter. He always seems to get it.*

Q. *Okay. You said that this stemmed from something about you dating white men. Is that because you dated a lot of white men, and the defendant didn't care for that?*

A. *Actually, I don't know how he ever knew who I was dating other than the fact that he would stand outside (my apartment building). The irony of all of this was the last person that I had had a date with was not white. He knew that. He had to have known because he was always watching.*

Q. *Did you see him watching?*

A. *No, but my dates would call me and say, "There is some guy standing outside your apartment building, and he looks like this." And I would know that it was him because I would then go to the window and, sure enough, there he is standing there. I remember on one occasion he asked one of my dates where we had gone and told him that, you know, he should stay away from me.*

Q. *Do you remember who that date was?*

A. *His name was Mike Schultz. He's at Harvard now. He's in law school. Then in the summer that happened again with someone that I had been dating.*

Q. *Okay. After the incident with your Miata like in June of '93,*

then what's the next thing that happened?
A. *The hang-ups continued.*

Q. *Did you have Caller ID or anything or did you just keep getting hang-up calls?*
A. *No, no. I have it now, but I didn't have it then.*

Q. *Okay.*
A. *That was about it. He was put in jail. My life got really quiet. And he was given — we went before Judge Mason and he was given two years' probation.*

Q. *What's the next thing that happened?*
A. *Well, it was quiet for a little while. Then the hang-ups started again. My friend, Ed, was getting these calls on Sunday mornings. His name is Ed Crony, if you want to talk to him.*

Q. *He works at the station with you?*
A. *Yes, Ed is in the Promotions department. He told me he was getting these calls on Sunday mornings that someone was looking for me. First of all, it was kind of odd that he would get these calls because he lives way up north (in the Kansas City metro area), and I have always lived down south. And we weren't dating. I had no reason to be at this place. I don't know where this person got his phone number, but there were some tell-tale signs in all of this. This person was looking for me. This person said that they knew for a fact I wasn't home and hadn't been and they desperately needed to find me. When Ed said, "Where are you calling from?" the person said, "From the television station. I work there." The reason that's a tell-tale sign is because we don't call it that. We call it "Four." Anybody in that building — we just don't refer to it so formally. It's work — the job. It's whatever. We just don't refer to it as the "television station." So Ed was savvy enough to ask a few questions. I don't remember verbatim what their conversation was. You can talk to Ed, but he seemed to think the caller thought there was a*

relationship going on between me and Ed. The caller would call on Sunday mornings, saying, "Where is she? Where was she?" Ed got the feeling that someone was trying to keep tabs on me via him. Also, my girlfriend Yalonda was getting hang-ups.

Q. You had told these people about what had been going on?
A. Oh, yeah. They're my closest friends.

* * * * *

Sunday nights have always been my favorite. The best program on television started at six, *60 Minutes,* followed by the second-best program, on a difference channel, of course, *The Simpsons.* The TV was loud, so I could hear over the sound of the dishwasher and washing machine. Sunday nights were pleasure and pain — TV and chores.

"This is *60 Minutes* with Lesley Stahl, Morley Safer, Ed Bradley ..." Hearing the opening credits inspired me to hurry along with my chores. I ran around the apartment collecting dirty clothes, towels and dishes. It was a contest. By the time the first in-depth report began, I had to be in place on the couch, a cup of hot tea in hand with my feet up.

After putting the last of the dishes in the dishwasher, I went over to the closet where my washer and dryer were. There were folding shutter doors that remained closed during the week to hide the machines. It was there, immediately after pulling back the door, that I saw it. A bottle of liquid Fab — not my brand, ever. My God — could it be? Had the stalker been here doing his laundry? I began to shake, tears flowing quickly — I felt so violated. I noticed an empty box of fabric softener sheets had been tossed in the open waste basket that sat just inside the laundry area. I knew I was alone because I'd just covered every square inch of it cleaning. When had he been there? Wiping my face on the sleeve of my flannel pajamas, I began moving the living room furniture against the door. He must have a key, I thought. I couldn't call the police. What would I tell them? This guy was really fucking with my head, and he somehow could come and go as he pleased. Just then, the phone rang.

"You're out of fabric softener." Click, he hung up. He knew my routine — laundry on Sunday nights. Detective Atwood was right. The next day I began looking for a new place to live.

During the housing search, the case regarding the break-in where the security guard was threatened went to trial. He went to jail. For more than two months my life was quiet. Things seemed to be returning to normal.

* * * * *

My new home was built in the 1930s by developer Napolean W. Dible. Dible became famous for his Tudor bungalow-style homes. Mine was the original Tudor, where Dible once lived. There were hundreds of the Tudors in and around a beautiful stretch of road called Ward Parkway. The road is divided by grassy areas which are dotted with fountains and clusters of flowers. Ward Parkway is home to the nation's first open-air shopping center, the Country Club Plaza, on its north end. There are dozens of mansions lining either side of the Parkway as you travel south from the Plaza. The farther south you go, the more modest the homes become, changing from mansions to Tudor homes to smaller cottage-type homes. Ward Parkway is easily the most recognizable street in Kansas City. It was perfect for my needs — an affordable older home in an area where many people were retired and stayed home a lot. The house was a private residence with an alarm on a major street. If anything happened, even at night, someone would be around — either in their home or driving on the Parkway.

* * * * *

Other than to my parents, Detective Atwood, the alarm company and the news director at work, I didn't give out my new phone number, so when the phone rang at three in the morning it almost had to be a call to cover a breaking news story, I thought.

"You can run, but you can't hide," he laughed. "Now, come on, you didn't think I'd let you out of my line of sight, did you?"

My throat seemed to close. I couldn't speak. The receiver felt like it was glued to my hand. I couldn't hang up, I was in shock.

"Heard your new place is great, right on the Parkway. You're one of the rich and famous now, huh? It's my place, too, you know. We both should be living there. It's just not right — you being in that big house all alone," the stalker said in a chillingly calm voice.

My fear turned to anger and determination. Remembering what Detective Atwood had told me about gathering information, I said, "How did you get this number?"

"I am the one with the power. I can do anything. Remember that the next time you try to hide. I know what I want to know because I know who to ask," he said proudly.

"Why are you doing this?" I asked.

"Oh, am I being interviewed now? You gonna do a news story on me? You know why — you have to love me, so we can be together for eternity." His voice seemed to change, it was not as deep or something. He sounded almost nervous … no, maybe surprised that I was talking to him.

"We will never be together." Anger was fueling me.

"Never say never. You thought I'd never get this number. You said I'd never see you again, and I'm anywhere I want to be. You just don't know when I'll show up," he quipped. "Or what I'll do."

I slammed down the receiver. Somehow he'd found me. Was there no escaping him? What would he do next? I'd lost control once again. But this time was different. So much about my life had been changed to avoid him, I felt like there was little or nothing more that I could do. I was at the mercy of the most merciless person I knew. That phone call to my new home sent me into a spiral of loneliness and despair. And something began to change inside me. I was desperate to have power over something, anything in my life.

Even my job was not in my control. Someone in upper management had decided the audience liked me enough to prompt my promotion to the evening anchor desk. But there was nothing tangible about my work — no product was constructed to be used at a later date — no measure of my ability other than the audience's response. And even that was not exact. Viewership of the evening news in Kansas City and many television markets is monitored by devices attached randomly to an unspecified number of TV sets. Some nights those devices showed that viewers preferred watching Channel 4. Other nights they preferred another station in town. It's a process known as ratings — the percentage of people watching a given station at a set time. There certainly was no way to control that.

And my personal life was upside down, changing constantly according to whatever crisis the stalker put into motion. But he couldn't manipulate everything. I discovered new ground to control — a discovery that led me down a self-destructive and dangerous path.

* * * * *

After another sleepless night, I lay in bed falling in and out of sleep under the cover of daylight. It was nearly noon, time to get dressed and get to work by one-fifteen. That would give me a chance to be in a seat for the daily editorial meeting that we used to construct the evening news.

Fortunately, my morning schedule was free of the community appearances I enjoyed making at area schools and charity events. On this day, I could at least get some sleep by allowing myself the luxury of staying in bed until it was absolutely necessary for me to be somewhere. I could sleep once the sun came out. The stalker rarely bothered me at home in the morning.

Along with my restlessness came a loss of appetite. At first, that was fine. Losing a few pounds was good for me. In fact, a girlfriend who wanted to lose weight talked me into joining a program with her. In a very short time, a weight loss counselor said I had reached my ideal weight in record speed. She said I should just maintain my weight by eating sensible portions of whatever I wanted. But it didn't stop there for me.

By controlling my food intake I felt some personal power. Some days I would eat fewer than 1,000 calories ... planning every bite of food that went into my mouth. Some days I ate nothing and just drank juice all day. Soon my once 5-foot-9-1/2-inch small-boned frame had gone from a slightly above ideal weight, 145 pounds, to a rail-thin 119 pounds. And the weight loss continued. People began to notice.

* * * * *

"Hey, Harris, did you see the overnight numbers from last night at ten?" the ten o'clock newscast producer asked. She and I were early for the editorial meeting. We sat in a couple of the dozen chairs around a large conference room table.

"No, how'd we do?" I asked.

"Well, we were number one. We crushed the competition!" she responded, bringing smiles from the reporters and others who were starting to file into the conference room. Quickly the seats filled up, leaving a couple of managers who showed up last to stand near the meeting room walls.

During this daily meeting, we go over the rundown of stories in the upcoming newscasts, beginning with the five o'clock broadcast. Reporters suggest story ideas, and we talk about the events of the day. It is a fast-paced and interesting discussion about the importance of different stories to our viewers. On that day, the Kansas City Chiefs football team was starting the pre-season at home. The plan was to have an anchor live at the stadium to jazz up the five and six o'clock newscasts with an extended look at the day's activities leading up to the seven o'clock kick-off.

Newsrooms often will send an anchor out into the field to cover a story when it's considered to have regional or national importance. For example, a jetliner crash or school shooting might be a story an anchor would cover live from the scene. The opening games of a new season in the National Football League can qualify as big stories for the home team cities. Kansas Citians love their NFL team. So on that day, I was assigned to do our live pre-game coverage at Arrowhead Stadium.

It was hot, nearly 100 degrees and even hotter on the stadium floor, which was then artificial turf. The turf has since been replaced with natural grass. Fortunately, I was prepared to go out into the field on a hot day or any other day, for that matter, because I kept casual clothes in my locker in the make-up room.

I left the meeting early to retrieve the clothes from the locker, and on my way down the hallway, away from the conference room, I looked back and noticed the news director and the manager of special projects talking just outside the meeting. As others began to exit the conference room, the two appeared to wrap up their quick conversation, and the special projects manager, Sindy Gaona, headed my way. Sindy was and remains the only woman manager in news at Channel 4. Some things about the TV news business are slow to change, and having women ascend to top management is one of them. However, the change is happening a bit quicker at some stations than others, especially in larger cities.

"Harris, wait before you get going. Can we talk for just a moment?" Sindy asked.

"Sure," I said. The photographer and I weren't leaving for the stadium for another half-hour, so she and I stepped into the small make-up room. It's a cramped space, with a mirror that runs the length of the room, about ten feet, and it starts at the ceiling and stops where it meets a long counter. There are electrical outlets all over for styling equipment and a sink in the center of the long counter. There's only one chair, which is really too large for the space. We stood alone in the room.

"I'm not sure how to put this," Sindy said, glancing at the floor, then back at me. "Can I be blunt?"

"Please," I answered.

"It's about your weight." Sindy paused, no doubt respecting the look of fear that crept across my face. "Are you eating? I mean, you've lost so much weight. Is everything okay?"

"I went on this diet and lost a few pounds. I just have a high metabolism," I said.

"Harris, it's very hot out today, and you don't look as strong as ... well, I'm concerned you may not have the stamina to stand out at the stadium for hours. But, more importantly, it can't be healthy for you. I've been asked to say something, the rest is up to you," she said. Sindy seemed frustrated that apparently I was in denial about the matter.

"Harris, we all go through things." She touched my arm. "Try not to take it all out on your body."

My eyes began to fill with tears. I wanted to tell her what was driving me to destroy my body, but I just couldn't admit that I was in trouble. I had to keep the stalking a secret. After all, this guy had once been a friend, someone I dated. What would people think? Would this manager and others lose respect for me because I'd made such a horrible mistake in my personal life? She truly looked worried about me. And throughout my ordeal, she was the only person to say anything to me about my dramatic weight loss.

I survived the heat at the stadium that day. But there were times when the stalker would cause such fear and unhappiness for me that the only way I felt I had any power in my life was to starve myself and exercise excessively. At times, I was rail thin. My eating disorder became the most severe when the stalker began to torment me in new ways. Again, after spending a couple of months behind bars, he had gotten my phone number and knew the neighborhood I'd moved to. It didn't stop there. He was determined to learn my new routine and try to regain control of my life, even though there was still a court order for him to stay away from me and he'd been arrested more than once. He was determined.

* * * * *

DEPOSITION (Continued ...)

Page 39
Mrs. Shostak, Public Defender, is holding photographs taken by Kansas City police and the USAA Insurance Company.

Witness (Harris Faulkner): It was parked outside my house. I didn't know he knew (exactly) where I lived until this happened. And he began jogging by my house. He (told police) he found out where I lived through the deed on my house.

Q. When did you move into your house?
A. In August of '93.

Q. So you didn't see anybody do this?
A. No.

Q. Did you call the police?
A. Oh, yeah.

Q. So who took this photo?
A. That (one) — USAA Insurance agency took that picture.

Q. I'm looking at a picture, a Polaroid, I guess. This is the passenger's side door?
A. Right.

Q. Okay. This is a black Miata?
A. Right.

Q. On the door is scratched "I suck white dick." (We'll get back to this.) After this incident in September of '93, did you ever have any more phone calls?
A. No more phone calls.

Q. You saw him jogging by your house — when?
A. I left for work every day between 1:00 and 1:15. I guess he must have been starting somewhere in the middle of Ward Parkway so he could time it, so he would jog by my house when I was coming out of the driveway. Well, when I called the police and told them this, they said, "Change your schedule." So I did and, sure enough, I was seeing him at a different point down the Parkway, and I had a cell phone. I would call them, and they never got him. There were always neighbors who saw him. They described that he had on purple shorts. He always had on the same thing. He had on purple shorts and a white T-shirt. That was the thing that made him so easy to spot, but yet the Kansas City, Missouri police officers couldn't spot him.

Q. So every time you saw him jogging he was wearing the same thing?

A. *Same thing.*

Q. *You clearly saw him? I mean, he would do this during the day?*
A. *He had his glasses on and everything, yeah. The whole thing for the police was, "Until he messes with you, the only thing we can do is observe." So I don't know. Maybe they did see him and they just didn't do anything ... I don't know if he just got tired. But I stopped seeing him jogging. I would say probably around Halloween '93 was the last time I saw him.*

Q. *Then what's the next time that you had a problem?*
A. *In November one morning in the wee hours of the morning I heard a loud noise outside, and it sounded like a thump on my roof. When I went out of my bedroom and into the hallway — there is a big plate glass window at the end of the hall — I walked up to the plate glass window, and there was somebody walking across my gravel bed, and I looked again and I recognized that it was (him). I went and called the police. I said, "Look. He is on my property. He's not supposed to be here. I've got an order of protection against him." By the time they got there, they couldn't find him. And the reason they couldn't find him was because he had been hanging out on the roof. That's probably why I heard the thump, but it took them a year to figure this out.*

Q. *Hanging out on the roof of your house?*
A. *Yeah. It wasn't until I guess he fell off or jumped off or whatever happened the (last time he was arrested) that police said, "Oh, well, maybe that's where he has been before." You know, who would look on somebody's roof?*

Q. *So he was just walking through your backyard?*
A. *He was kicking the rocks out of my gravel bed. He was making noise which was kind of weird, enough noise to wake me up. He looked up at me in the window. I had no voice. I was just shaking from head to toe.*

Q. Okay. When you had the incident in November when he was going through the gravel, was there anybody else in your house with you at the time?
A. No.

Q. — Or were you the only one home?
A. Right.

Q. What was the next time that you had something happen?
A. It was quiet the month of December and most of January. And I started getting hang-ups again.

Q. And nothing was said once you picked up the phone?
A. Nothing.

Q. You said that you had changed your phone number a number of times. Have you always been unlisted?
A. Oh, always, yeah … I would get a lot of calls if my schedule had changed. For instance, if I came home at 1:00 in the morning one night because I worked late, I would get a call. If I came home the next night at 11:30 like I always do, I wouldn't get a call. If there was something different about my pattern — it was like I was being monitored.

Q. Okay. After the hang-up calls, did you have any other incident?
A. I started dating someone. He's a personal trainer (at my health club). His name is Paul. I didn't tell Paul about any of this. It's kind of hard to meet somebody and say, "Oh, by the way, I'm being stalked." We had only gone out a couple of times, and I really didn't think it was necessary to show him photos and such. I don't want people to think of me as a victim all the time, so Paul didn't know to look out for this person, but (the defendant) approached him at the gym. Paul had his headset on. He had followed Paul there and asked him if he knew anybody famous. Paul said, "Like Joe Montana?" (The defendant) said, "No, you know who I'm talking about." Paul thought for a minute and said, "Harris?" (The defendant) smiled and warned Paul to stay away from me.

When I talked to Paul after that, he said, "Hey, what's going on? Who is this?" I told him all about it. He said, "Well, I don't like the fact I'm being followed. What's the deal with this? Am I in any danger?" So at that time I hired a private investigator to (prove) who was writing on my cars and just to help me solve what was going on and to keep it from happening. (The investigator) talked to Paul and showed him the picture of (the defendant), and he fingered him. He said, "Yeah, that's the guy."

Q. You said that he had followed Paul?

A. Right. The day before that happened, Paul and I had given each other a hug in the (health club) parking lot. I know that it wasn't a coincidence. Also, following the hug in the parking lot, my car was etched the next day.

Q. So the same thing happened (with your car) again.

A. The very next day. Only this time on the front passenger door on the bigger car it said, "I'm a sell-out."

Q. After it happened to your car the first time, you got that fixed?

A. Yeah.

Mr. Rieg, Jackson Co. Prosecutor: Excuse me for interrupting. Two different cars?

The Witness: Two different cars. One was four-door. That's why there were two doors on the passenger's side.

Q. (By Ms. Shostak): So the first time it happened to your Miata?

A. Yeah.

Q. Then this happened again, a year later? July of '94?

A. Right. It happened to a purple-colored Millennia that I had been driving that I was thinking about buying that still had dealer plates on it and did not belong to me.

Q. That said what? I'm sorry?

A. On the front passenger door it said, "I'm a sell-out." On the back passenger door it said —

Q. *"I suck white dick." Okay. You didn't see anybody do that at the time?*

A. *No, but a guy fitting the defendant's description was walking — was seen walking by a police officer and getting on a bus just moments before I called 911. So there was a cop down there.*

Q. *How is it you know that?*

A. *Because he answered my call. There was a cop down the hill who observed him. He thought it was kind of strange because he had seen (a man) walking through the parking lot kind of catty-cornered, so he watched him walk down the hill and get on the bus just to ID this guy in case something had happened. Moments after that, I had called 911 from the club. He's the one who was dispatched to my call. He said, "I just saw this guy."*

Q. *So this was done while your car was parked at the health club?*

A. *Yes.*

Q. *Okay, so you made a report then again on that incident?*

A. *Oh, yeah.*

Q. *Is that as far as that ever went?*

A. *No. It's a felony because the damage was over $1500. Police started looking into the case. They wanted to know — I mean, basically it's a different state — Kansas. So you start all over again. They wanted a chronology of everything that happened in Missouri. The number that was listed for him when he ran a check on him was Public Defender Mary Clark's number, so (a detective) called her to find out if that was where he was living, and she said yes and he wasn't home at the time. He told her, "Look, there could be some charges on this guy, and we need to know where he was." She swore up and down that she had no idea where he was at that time. Then, after that he just never returned to that house, according to her. This is all per a Kansas Detective Dahmer.*

* * * * *

The summer of 1994, more than one year after the nightmare had begun, I was being stalked in two states — both sides of the Kansas City metro area — Missouri and Kansas. There was no place I could go that the stalker couldn't find me. He would do terrible things, writing obscene messages on my car, threatening me and anyone close to me, and the police said they could not catch him. And even if they could find him, officers told me that they needed to either catch him in the act of doing something or I would have to suffer some violent act before he'd do serious time behind bars.

Detective Atwood had talked with me about that stalker growing more bold in his actions, terrorizing me in public places in broad daylight. And it was very disturbing to learn that he had been getting help or at least a place to live for free, from a woman who had once represented him for trespassing charges early in his pursuit of me. No wonder he was so effective in his quest to make my life hell. Without bills to pay, he could spend all of his time stalking me. And who else besides a public defender had helped him sustain?

And the legal system helped him, too. Once before Judge Mason in Jackson County court, the stalker was praised for being well dressed and I was scolded for being so popular I must be driving men mad! A judge said that in an open courtroom. It was my fault this man was after me? Clearly the stalker had some advantages both in how the law worked and in some people's attitudes toward women and, in my case perhaps, their attitudes toward successful women.

My mind and body were tired. A sense of hopelessness washed over me. When would it all end? So much had happened. At the start, in the spring of 1993, the stalker said he wanted us to be in love, to spend the rest of our lives together. When I would not play a part in that fantasy, he came up with a new one. His next fantasy was that he would tear apart my life, cause me to lose my job, my house, my dreams — everything. Repeatedly in phone messages left on my answering machine, he would say how he looked forward to the day when I would have to depend on him to rescue me.

When that didn't happen, the stalker took a new tack, threatening violence and carrying out violent acts to control me. He said that he would scar my face so no one else would want me. He said death would follow. His so-called life-long love for me had turned to hate. His hatred was a weird mixture of moments of twisted joy from watching me suffer and unpredictable rage from watching me survive.

It was puzzling why the stalker didn't just kill me — carry out his threats rather than torturing me. More than once, I thought of ending my life so he couldn't. Ready to say good-bye to the emotional pain, I tried to prepare myself to say good-bye to the people I loved. How would they handle such a death? I couldn't disgrace my family in that way. Yet, surviving seemed to be growing beyond my strength and control. Some days I found the thought of stepping outside my front door unbearable, but somehow there was the courage to face another day. It was as though it were coming from something else.

With each bad thing that would happen at the hands of a hateful man, there would be a blessing, a moment of joy, usually joy that I caused in someone else's life. A story that I would cover for the evening news would bring a new person into my life who needed to see or hear that story. Or maybe it was a public appearance at which I spoke and somehow magically said just the right thing to the crowd. The thought of being able to make a positive difference in the lives of people around me kept me going. And there was the effect that people had on me. Like the woman who got me to do the one thing that may have saved me from destroying myself.

* * * * *

The order of protection papers that made it illegal for the stalker to walk onto my home or work property or to come near me had to be renewed every 180 days. I was required to appear in court before a judge to petition the renewal based on incidents of threats or abuse. Basically, the papers allowed police to arrest the stalker should they catch him anywhere near me, although the punishment usually was only probation or a few nights in the Jackson County jail. But keeping the papers up to date was critical because, without them, there would be no consequences for him pursuing me unless he was caught destroying property or attacking me.

Going to court was so humiliating. People recognized me from the evening news. And while they were nice and often concerned, their stares and whispers were hurtful. What did they think of seeing a prominent person in the community petitioning for help against a man she'd once dated? Did they think less of me? Had I let them down by becoming a story instead of just telling them stories on the news?

My mind was filled with these questions as I stood before Judge Christine Sill-Rogers. A nice lady with dark hair peppered with gray streaks. Her smile was warm, yet she seemed in control, strong. She had seen me in her courtroom once before, getting the orders of protection papers renewed. She always began the process by explaining the procedure. I was the petitioner and the stalker was called the respondent in this courtroom. In her chambers, the judge had previously reviewed the case along with other cases on her docket that day. She had the sole responsibility of deciding whether the petitioner was in danger. If so, the judge would sign off on the renewal and the respondent would be served with the petition for renewal. That would put into effect another six months of legal protection for me.

On this day, the judge quickly looked over the paperwork again. I stood before her in silence. The stalker was not in court. But the courtroom was filled with other petitioners, mostly women, trying to protect themselves from domestic abusers and others. One woman in particular was seated in the row of pews directly behind me.

She whispered, "Is that you, the lady on the news?" She smiled. I turned around to see her face, bruised on one side. Her mouth was swollen on that same side. Someone must have hit her several times.

"Yes," I whispered back, trying to force a smile.

"Oh, you don't have to fake it for me, sister. I know you're in pain — some kind of trouble. That's why we're all here. You're no different from the rest of us," she said softly. Her voice consoled me. She understood.

The judge continued to look over the paperwork before her.

The woman behind me spoke again. "Who's after you? Somebody who saw you on TV?"

"No, I dated this guy a long time ago. Not too bright, I guess. No taste in men," I said, in jest.

"It's not your fault you ran into some freak. Happens to some of us more than once in a lifetime. But you know whatcha gotta do, don't-chu?" she asked.

"Do? I'm here doing the legal thing," I responded.

The woman leaned forward and motioned for me to come closer to her.

The judge was not ready to proceed with my petition yet, so I moved closer to the woman. She held out her right hand, which had been resting beneath a sweater on her lap. She had a cast on that hand, but she held it out anyway to grab my fingers with hers that wiggled free from the end of the cast. We hooked fingers.

"You look so much younger off the TV and in person. You're just a kid," she said, surprised. She looked to be in her early forties.

"There's only one thing for you to do with somebody who's hurting you. You have to pray to God for the strength to survive. And you have to ask him to show you something good that can come out of it." She looked deeply into my eyes. "Now you're going to be fine. Just keep fighting and looking as good as you do on TV. I'll be watching. And remember, you gotta pray."

"Thank you," I said. The noises inside the courtroom seemed to fade for the moment that she was speaking. All I could hear were her words, and all I could see were her eyes. For a few seconds, I had found peace. Something solemn but sturdy hung like an angel's aura around this woman's face — not literally — it was just a feeling I got. It was like she had discovered a safe, peaceful space within herself and was sharing that with me.

The judge interrupted us ...

IN THE CIRCUIT COURT OF JACKSON COUNTY, MISSOURI
AT KANSAS CITY, DIVISION 107
Harris Faulkner, Petitioner   vs.   Respondent
No. DR 94-8666
FULL ORDER OF PROTECTION
Adult Abuse
September 22, 1994
*JUDGE CHRISTINE SILL-ROGERS. This court hears the petition
to renew a full order of protection against the respondent. I am
signing this petition, granting the request for renewal. Again, this
court orders the respondent not to abuse, threaten to abuse, mo-
lest, stalk or disturb the peace wherever the petitioner may be.*

* * * * *

When life was easier, prayer was too. Asking God to help me
realize my dreams of being a TV journalist seemed so long ago
and so simple compared to the situation before me now. I knew
about praying for good fortune, but not about surviving the tough
times. Why didn't God just help me? Was his power only for those
who wore the scars of pain? Maybe God only helped people
who had bruises. Maybe my fear and pain were so well hidden
that even He couldn't see them. Pray, one more time. Why not?
On my knees just like that woman said, I prayed not to end the
situation, but for the strength to endure it. If there was something to be done or a mission to follow, I prayed that God please
show me.

* * * * *

"Harris Faulkner, please come to the front lobby. Harris
Faulkner, please come to the front lobby." I left the late afternoon bustle of the newsroom, went down the stairs in the front
building, and as I reached the last few steps, there he was, his
back to me.

"Harris, I paged you because you have a visitor. Here, sir,

please sign in here," the receptionist handed the man a pen. He signed his name on the visitor's registry and turned to greet me.

"Harris, I stopped by —"

"Oh, hey, Gary, what's up?" I was relieved and glad to see this man. He was the private investigator I'd hired to find out more about the stalker and to see if he could help catch him. Gary Towns specialized in personal protection, a fancy way of saying he was a bodyguard. He had worked for diplomats, celebrities, housewives, just about anyone who could afford him. It took every penny in my savings to acquire his services, but it proved to be worth it.

"Harris, is there some place we can talk?" Gary asked. "Oh, before I go, Janice was it?" Gary leaned over the large lobby desk.

"Yes," Janice smiled.

"Remember what I told you, keep that notebook and pen right here, so that everyone who's not an employee must sign in," Gary warned. "And remember, be nosy. Ask these people questions. They're strangers and you're the station's first line of defense."

"Oh, nothing ever happens around here," Janice said, smiling at Gary as she picked up an incoming phone line.

Gary and I went into a small conference room just off the lobby. He closed the door, and we sat in the large, cushy chairs around a table. He took out some papers from the briefcase he had been carrying.

"First things first. Harris, you have no protection here. That receptionist didn't even ask whether I had business at the station. She simply told me to sit and wait while she called one of the station's most recognizable people down to talk with me. I'm a complete stranger. They're not security serious here at all. And for you, that's a problem — a very bad problem."

Gary was a tough-looking man, in his early forties. He took his work seriously. And he dressed sort of like a commando. He had a lot of light brown hair, cut in long layers that grew just below his ears. He wore dark glasses, even indoors. And no matter what shirt and pants he was wearing, he always wore a military-style vest like a jacket over his shirt. The vest was filled with pockets, one of which no doubt held the weapon with which he was armed. Unconventional looking, but strong and sure of himself. He had an air of confidence that put some people, like the receptionist Janice, at ease and set others back on their heels. Gary used to tell me the innocent people are not threatened by his authoritative presence, while those who have something to hide are always bothered by him. He said that's how he could tell the good from the bad, an advantage in his line of investigative and security work, he said.

"I don't know. The station seems pretty secure to me. There are always people around. And I've been so afraid to stay at home at nights, I've spent a few here in the bigger conference room upstairs. I mean, there's no way he'd guess to find me here at that time. So no hang-ups to keep me worried and awake at night," I explained.

"Harris, this guy is closer to you than you know. I met with a Detective Atwood down at Kansas City, Missouri, police headquarters about your case today. Pleasant fellow and one who's definitely concerned about your well being. I shared with him what I've been able to find out about the guy who's been tormenting you. And, I don't want to frighten you, but there are some things you should know. That's why I'm here now, in the middle of your work day —"

"Oh, that's okay, Gary. I don't go on the air for another hour. I have time to listen. And Atwood's already given some details and advice," I said.

"Good. Here's what's new. And I should say what I'm about to tell you has the police turning over their case to the prosecutor's office. They say this guy could be the first to be in Jackson County court on Missouri's new stalking law. And yeah, I've got an ego, so being a part of this is a thrill for me." Gary was organizing his notes as he talked.

"Okay, here goes. We've been wondering how he knows your work schedule, like when you're out in the field or what hours you're actually in the building. Check this out. This guy's enrolled himself at school at the community college across the street." Gary seemed proud to be able to supply me with such detailed information, but he was terrifying me.

"You mean Penn Valley Community College?" My voice was shaking.

"Yeah. And get this, one of his professors has been on alert, notifying his superiors at the college about this guy in his class. The guy who's been stalking you wrote about you in one of his papers, saying you're going to be married soon. He bragged to that professor about being able to watch the Channel 4 parking lot from the campus. I interviewed this professor," Gary continued.

"But how can he be going to a junior college? In North Carolina he'd said he went to college already," I said.

"Yeah, well, he's going all over again just to be near you. Harris, no more sleeping at this television station. And certainly don't stay here late at night at all, until they hire some professional security for the place," Gary said sternly.

"Well, no one knows when I stay here but the cleaning crew —"

"Wrong! He knows you're here. I'll prove it. Where are these cleaning people?"

"What? Where are the janitors who work at this building?"

"Well, they work at night. I think they start in the evenings, maybe in another couple of hours. Why?" I asked.

"I've gone to the liberty of running off some copies of a photograph of this guy. My bet is your co-workers and others around you are seeing him constantly, maybe even talking with him, without even knowing it," Gary said.

"No way," I said.

"Harris, it's time for you to blow the whistle to everyone about this. I know you've told your co-anchor, Phil Witt, and a couple of the managers, but you can't hide it any more. If this guy's looking for an opportunity to befriend a co-worker or a janitor to get into this building —"

"But this place is safe. We're the 24-hour newschannel. People are always here," I said.

"He's getting closer. With that restraining order of protection against him, he knows he can't just walk up on the property repeatedly. So instead he positions himself across the street where he can see everyone coming and going. He sees who you're close to, who you go to dinner with. He sees when the building is mostly full and when it's nearly empty. And he knows when you don't go home at night. It's just a matter of time before he walks through that front door and friendly Janice or an unsuspecting janitor leads him right to you," Gary said.

Gary reminded me that the stalker had been armed with a knife during at least one other incident — like I needed to be reminded. Gary stayed with me during my shift that evening. He was introduced to the station's management. He met with the general manager and the news director, talking with them about my situation and the lack of security in the building. He told them he was hired to protect me and that meant he'd need to talk with employees like the overnight cleaning crew. Gary canvassed the building showing the stalker's picture to every employee.

* * * * *

"That's going to do it for us tonight. Join us for news at ten tomorrow night," Phil Witt said. The ten o'clock news was wrapping up.

"Until then, have a good one," I said. The newscast ended, and my co-anchor, Phil, and I removed our microphones from our suit lapels.

"Harris, is that Gary guy here to walk you out to your car every night now?" Phil was looking over at Gary who had positioned himself so he could watch the news set, where Phil and I sat, the camera crew and the stage door. Gary never relaxed. He just stood.

"Yeah, and he's been talking with people in the building to see if anyone has seen the stalker," I said.

"Hey, you know if you need anything, Kim and I are there

for you. And the kids would love to see you." Phil put his arm around my shoulder.

"Thanks so much, Phil. You're such a good friend. I'm glad you're here for me," I said, as we walked out of the studio. Gary followed close behind. After gathering my purse and make-up bag and jacket, I was escorted to my car. Gary said he'd stick around the station parking lot to see if he saw anyone around who might try to follow me home, and then he would arrive at my house to make sure I got inside safely. There was a knock at the back door a few minutes after I got home.

"Harris, it's just Gary. Everything all right in there?" I opened the door, and Gary stood in the back doorway for just a moment.

"Yes, I'm fine. And the alarm was still activated, so no one has tampered with anything here. What did you find out today from showing the picture around?" I asked. Gary seemed different, worried.

"Oh, kiddo. We'll talk about it tomorrow. You just get some sleep. I'm going to stay parked outside in your driveway tonight. So don't you worry about anything." Gary took out his cellular phone.

"All night?" I asked.

"Yep. I'm calling my wife now to let her know to expect a husband home at dawn with a sore back." Gary smiled. What had he discovered that had him keeping watch like this? With him in the driveway, at least I could fall asleep.

* * * *

The next day was beautiful. The end of summer in Kansas City is breathtaking, with all of the leaves on the older trees turning golden and the first bit of chill in the air. It was one of the last days of the year that I could ride around with the convertible top down on my Miata. To keep warm, I wore a leather bomber jacket over my suit. Driving down ward Parkway, I put in Janet Jackson's CD and sang along with my favorite song, "That's the Way Love Goes." Gary had me invest in a cellular phone so that I could contact him whenever I was on the move. So I phoned him to let him know my first stop was at an elementary school for its career day. He said he'd be waiting for me in the parking lot at work. Students asked me all sorts of questions about being in TV news, running me past my expected arrival time at work. As I pulled into the parking lot, Gary seemed to appear out of nowhere in a car behind me, following me to a parking space. As I got out of my car, I noticed a patrol car parked near the station's back door.

"Hey, Gary, sorry I'm a little late. But you didn't have to call the cops," I said, smiling.

"I was going to call your cell phone in a few minutes to check on you. That officer is here for another reason," Gary said. He walked with me to the back door. We paused before going inside to watch the policeman who was in his car talking on a hand-held radio. We could hear the sound of his voice because his door was open. He sat with one leg hanging out of the car with his foot resting on the ground. He was writing something on a notepad.

"Remember, I began showing the photo of the stalker to employees here late yesterday. Well, I came back early this morning to catch that shift, and the results of my efforts were part of the reason your station management has asked local authorities for a bit of increased security until we catch this guy," Gary explained.

"You mean people have seen him on the property?" I asked.

"Seen him, talked to him, as recently as yesterday morning. The stalker went to the front door of the station looking for you, and when he was told you were not in yet, he asked the receptionist your schedule. Fortunately, she didn't know the answer to that and asked him to leave. But he didn't give up. He went to the back door, and someone saw him trying to get in. When confronted, he said he was looking for directions to the nearest gas station. The employee who talked with him said he left suddenly, not waiting to hear the directions. And he left on foot," Gary said.

"But the restraining order says he's not supposed to be anywhere near my workplace," I said.

"Your schedule has been sporadic lately with all your community appearances. Looks like he's having a tough time keeping up," Gary said.

"Is that all? You said that was part of the reason the cops are here?"

"This morning he crossed a line no one could have predicted. He called your general manager demanding that the station take you off the evening news. He obviously does not like all the attention your growing popularity is bringing. He wants you off TV in a hurry," Gary said.

"Did he threaten the general manager?"

"Harris, the station called the police — I didn't."

"Oh, my God."

"The management will talk with you about this more. But just so you know, the police officers think it's a good idea for you to stay on the air. It sends the message that you are strong against this guy's demands. But that's ultimately up to you." Gary pointed to the officer. "That's a senior detective out in that patrol car. We're all working off the same page now. And the common thought is this — something's shifted this guy into the next gear. I work for you, and I won't leave your side unless you tell me to back off." Gary seemed validated in his cause. And he was more focused than ever.

A shift in the stalker's behavior. Now the station management was a target. My theory was that the stalker was angry about changes in my life. He no doubt noticed that I was seldom alone, between the private investigator and people I was surrounded by at community appearances. To him it must have looked like he was being completely eliminated from my life.

And then there were the changes in me. During a six-week self-defense training course, I'd begun to lift weights and eat healthily. Dealing with my eating disorder was made easier by concentrating on being physically strong. My friends noticed my posture and even the way I walked exuded more confidence. Although fear and confusion dwelled in my head, my outside appearance could fool anybody — maybe even the stalker.

His response was to send messages to me that he was still around: calling the station management, being seen by employees who could describe him, and there were strange occurrences at my home.

Upon returning home from work late at night, often I'd find my wrought iron patio furniture stacked up against the house, one piece on top of the other. Some of that furniture weighed 70 pounds or more. There would be times when the exterior lights would be out. He would unscrew the light bulbs or cut electrical wires to leave the driveway and backyard in complete darkness, and it meant the electric garage door would not work by remote.

Once he broke into the detached garage and placed that heavy patio furniture in a line from inside the garage all the way to the back door, forcing me to have to deal with a bizarre mess in the dark. There was a time when those weird things would have terrified me, but again there were changes in my life. Hiring Gary was a smart move. His idea of telling co-workers and neighbors to look out for this guy apparently encouraged many of them to take their own action. For instance, the neighbors around me would leave their backyards lit up brightly so my driveway was never completely dark, no matter what the stalker did.

* * * * *

DEPOSITION (Continued ...)

Page 77

Q. (By Ms. Shotak, Public Defender): Sometimes you came home and your gate was open and your alarm system was constantly going off?

A. (By Witness, Harris Faulkner): Yeah. It was being set off in different areas of the house, meaning it wasn't a rodent or something small getting up against the basement windows. It was different areas of the house, so somebody was tampering with it. Generally, it would happen while I was on the air. When the newscast would end, I'd be told the alarm company had called and police were at my house. It kept happening. And I would go home and stuff would be moved around. My gates opened and my porch furniture would be moved around.

* * * * *

We never learned why the stalker set off the house alarm, but it was speculated that perhaps he was trying to annoy the neighbors, drive them to a point where they would no longer want to come to my aid. It didn't work. But all of this behavior was working for me and my mission. God had answered my prayers and showed me how to survive. Detective Atwood, the private investigator Gary Towns, police officers and the Jackson County prosecutor's office had mentioned Missouri's new anti-stalking law. They told me no one was challenging it. Victims were too afraid to meet their tormentors in court, and prosecutors couldn't win cases without the victims' help. God put it on my heart to be the first to challenge that law in Kansas City. To do that, the stalker had to show a pattern of pursuits and threats over an extended period of time that were witnessed by others and could be documented. He was doing that — playing right into the hands of the law.

* * * * *

"I'm not taking no for an answer. We've planned this trip for a long time," my mother was determined. She and my father were on separate phones at their home in Dallas. We'd been on the phone long distance for more than an hour. My dad wanted to know every detail about the increased stalking incidents of late. And he pressed for an explanation about why that was a good thing. I explained what authorities had told me. The stalker was displaying a pattern of abuse, and he was showing up in places he could easily be caught. My parents were concerned about my money situation. Did I have enough cash to keep the private investigator-turned-bodyguard at my side? My dad said to let them know the minute I needed anything. And my mother insisted on coming to stay with me. She said she'd been looking forward to the trip and wanted to be with me in case they happened to catch the stalker at my home.

"Oh, Mom. He's been here a thousand times and they haven't caught him. It will never happen like that. He'll stay away now that I have someone protecting me," I argued.

"I don't think so. Call it mother's intuition or whatever. I just have a feeling." My mother is one of the most level-headed people I know. She does very little based on emotions or impulse. And talking about intuition was not like her at all. She reasoned that she could comfort me while the police stepped up their efforts to catch the stalker. And no matter what havoc he was causing, she was not canceling her trip. She was coming to Kansas City and that was that.

She arrived on Friday, September 9th. With a night off from work, I was able to spend a quiet evening with her. We talked and laughed over dinner. Before we went to sleep that night, I checked outside and there was Gary, parked in the driveway as he was every night from eleven to dawn. I waved from my bedroom window, and he waved back. My phone rang.

"Everything all right in there?" Gary was making his usual final call of the day.

"Oh, yeah. You know, I was thinking. You're here so much without a break — why don't you take tomorrow and Sunday night off? My mom is here, and we'll be turning in early every night. We can just check in with each other by phone and, of course, I'll call 911 if anything happens," I said.

"Well, I do have another case I could work on over this weekend, and maybe I could take my wife out for dinner. But we'll keep in touch by phone every few hours — that's a must. Now get some sleep," Gary said.

* * * * *

The next day, my mom and I shopped like time was running out on earth. That was great therapy for me. Mom was right, she was a comfort at a time when I needed it most.

That night some friends had invited me to go dancing. Initially, I declined the offer, but my mom said I should go out and have some fun — get my mind off the negative things in my life.

She said that she'd wait up for me, and I agreed to be home shortly after midnight.

My friends and I headed to Westport, Kansas City's nightclub district. A Saturday night out having fun. It had been too long since I'd experienced that. And I took full advantage, dancing nonstop with our group of seven. We were all over the dance floor. We literally bumped into a friend of mine, Alex Lepper, who was a police officer. He was off duty that night. Alex joined us. After a few songs, we danced our way off the floor and began crowding into a booth. Some of my friends ordered drinks, and Alex and I sat and talked.

I was telling Alex about how much fun my mother and I were having while she was in town. As I looked across the dance floor, watching the faces of others in the nightclub enjoying themselves, I saw him. The stalker was across the room watching us. Alex grabbed my hand and told me and my friends to leave the bar immediately. Alex and I had met one night when he and another officer responded to a 911 call at my home. Alex knew the stalker was dangerous. We left through the front door of the nightclub, and Alex went his own way — alerting some policemen who were working the Westport walkways for crowd control. My friends had carpooled, and I had driven alone. They needed to make several stops, and it made more sense for me just to go straight home. My mother would be waiting for me. It was just after midnight.

Somehow, the stalker beat me to my house. When he saw the lights were on, he must have assumed I was inside. He had been knocking on the doors, trying to taunt whoever was there. As I pulled into the driveway, I noticed the wrought iron gates were open. I had left them closed. Perhaps my mother had opened them for some reason, I thought. Quickly making my way into the back door, I found my mother inside shaking in fear. She had called 911, but hung up ... thinking maybe she'd imagined the banging noises on the doors and windows. Just then, I heard something at the back door. It wasn't locked. In my haste, the door was left unlocked. I ran to turn the dead-bolt. There he was standing on the porch — grinning.

He mouthed the words, "I gotcha now." We both reached for the door knob at the same time. I managed to push in the button lock and ran to another part of the house, grabbing my cell phone. I called 911 back, and they said the hang-up earlier had prompted the dispatcher to send officers out. At the front door, my mother and I watched him trying to get into the house.

"Where are you going?" my mother asked. I was running up the stairs to my bedroom.

"I'm going to get my gun." I rounded the corner of the door and went straight to the left side of my bed. Under the pillow on that side lay my hand gun — loaded and ready to fire. As I put my hand on the cold metal, I heard my mother call out.

"No! Harris, the police are on their way. It's their battle now. Let them deal with this maniac! Please don't —"

I let go of the gun and covered it back up with the pillow. My mother was waiting for me at the bottom of the stairs. I returned to her empty-handed.

"Don't you see, if you shoot him, then you have to live with that memory and maybe worse if he doesn't die." She was strangely calm. And what she said made sense.

I never wanted to use that gun and, unless he found a way into the house, I wouldn't. That was the agreement she and I struck. We huddled together and had started to walk into the kitchen, when we saw the stalker had returned to the front porch. He was pacing. He turned and looked through the round, lattice-paned window that was in the center of the front door. Again, he was grinning, just like he had been at the back door. It was as though he knew what was going to happen and we were at his mercy.

"The police are coming!" I screamed. Telling Gary Towns to take the night off because my mom was in town was a huge mistake.

"Harris, let me in. I'm at the back door. It's Gary." Pulling the back door drapes to the side, I peeked and saw Gary on the porch. He was wearing his vest, loaded down with what looked like ammunition and carrying a gun. "Are you and your mother all right?" I opened the door and let him in. We closed the door behind him.

"Gary, what are you doing here? How did you know?"

"Harris, I've got a scanner in the car. And just as a precaution, I thought I'd drive through your neighborhood on my way from another surveillance job. When I heard police cars being dispatched to this area — here I am. You must be Shirley?"

"Yes, I'm Harris' mom. Glad you're here. It sounds like the police are here, too," my mother said. We heard sirens and then silence. Then, footsteps to the back porch. A policeman knocked at the door. Gary let him in.

"Miss Faulkner, we're here. One of your neighbors spotted this guy. We have every available officer in the area looking for him. Mr. Towns, you got here fast."

The officer and Gary had worked some other crime scene together. Now we were all standing in my kitchen — me, my mom, Gary and this officer. Gary went around the house checking the locks on all the windows and doors. The officer stayed in the kitchen talking with the policemen on his walkie-talkie.

"Yeah, everything's quiet here. The two women are fine," the officer said into the device.

When Gary returned to the kitchen, he said he had an idea. In his investigation he had spoken with the neighbors in the house directly behind mine. They told him about hearing noises in their backyard at night and that their dogs would sometimes suddenly bark non-stop. He motioned to the officer to follow him out the back door.

Gary's hunch was right. The stalker was perched on top of the neighbors' detached garage which was adjacent to my detached garage. He could jump from building to building and hide on their property. But he didn't jump. When Gary and the officers shone a light up there, the stalker panicked and fell over backward, hitting the neighbors' basketball rim on his way down. He was hurt, but he kept running.

About 15 minutes after he fell, the stalker was caught. His face was bloodied from what police called the garage accident.

And one of his hands was cut badly. It turned out he had broken into the mailbox slot that went into my home and was cut by the metal as he pulled his hand out. They discovered my phone bill and tube of lipstick in his pockets. He apparently had gone through my trash as well.

* * * * *

The prosecutor, C.J. Rieg, told me we now had a strong case against the stalker. She filed misdemeanor stalking charges in Jackson County. We waited six months for the case to go to trial.

On March 5, 1995, we were told that with testimony the trial could take a couple of days. It didn't. On the first day, the stalker sat at a courtroom table a few feet across from the prosecution's stable. I sat behind the prosecutor on the benches where courtroom visitors sat. My friend, Jeni Cardin, was with me. I didn't look at him, but he was watching me. I later learned that on that day the stalker had made comments about the way I looked with my new haircut and how I smelled from across the room.

On the second day of trial we entered the courtroom and heard the news. The public defender had advised him to plead guilty to the stalking charges. Since he'd been waiting in jail, the judge invoked a four-month suspended sentence and placed him on three years' probation. He also had to complete a psychiatric program and be remanded to the custody of his family who attended the trial and returned with him to their home in Pennsylvania.

* * * * *

"I know it doesn't feel like it, but we won," C.J. said. "If he contacts you again, his probation will be revoked and he'll go to prison because that will be a felony. It's not the best ending, but it is an ending."

CHAPTER TWO

Shaking the Shadow

LOOK BEHIND YOU, over each shoulder. When the phone rings, imagine it's someone who wants to harm you. When you climb into bed at night, lie awake worrying about every creaking piece of wood in your home, every sound of bushes blowing in the wind outside and every noise you can't identify. Now, start over and do it all again. That was my life for months after the trial ended.

The stalker hadn't won, but he had done some damage. No longer was there a private investigator to watch over me. My closest friends and co-workers had moved on with their lives. And even my family had stopped calling daily to check on me. For the first time in a long time, I was alone. Yet something was keeping me company like a shadow — something bad. It was fear. How would I return to normal life, doing things on my own at any time I wanted? Would I be safe? If I befriended another man and dated him, would he turn out to be a stalker? Or would being on television make me a target of a random pursuer? Who could I trust?

Oddly enough, the first person to hint that there would be long-lasting effects of being stalked was the defense attorney in the final moments of the pre-trial deposition. It was her job to defend the stalker, but she undoubtedly was getting to know him. Maybe somehow those last questions were a subliminal slip that she knew what I had gone through.

* * * * *

DEPOSITION (Continued)

Page 78

Q. (By Mrs. Shotak, Public Defender): Have you had to — have

*you gotten any type of treatment or seen any doctors or any-
thing over any of this? Have you gone to any counseling or
gotten any therapy:*

A. *(By Witness, Harris Faulkner): Oh, no. I think, you know, I
am very blessed. I have people in my life — my mom was with
the state of California for years (as a counselor), so I talk to my
mom, but not in a medical capacity really. She just loves me.
The only thing that I have done is to hire a private investigator
who was part bodyguard because I was afraid for my life.*

Q. *Okay.*

A. *So, that's it. We (my mother and I) were talking about my love
life this morning. The long-term effect of this is that I don't — I
don't trust. I mean, I'm afraid to get close to people. Now you
may think I need counseling because of that, but that's the effect that it has, and I guess I'll deal with that as best I can.*

Q. *Okay. You continue to date people?*

A. *I had stopped for a while, and I started again this summer. Not
every guy can handle this scenario. It's a point of control that
somebody else has in your life, and not everybody can deal
with that.*

Q. *Is there anything else that you can remember that you want to
add to any of the questions I have asked before?*

A. *No.*

* * * * *

As the public defender wrapped up the deposition, she said
something quietly in the ear of her assistant. They exchanged a
strange concerned look. The public defender had that same look
on her face after the trial. What did she know about the stalker?
The answer to that question still haunts me. But moving on with
my life and shaking the shadow of fear was part of God's plan
for my life.

* * * * *

October 13, 1995 — Seven months and one week after the

trial ended, I turned 30. My friends threw me a huge party at a local Greek restaurant. Opening presents and cards was great fun. I got some interesting napkin rings. Perhaps one of my friends got me confused with our friend who was having a housewarming party later that week. One card stuck out. Inside it read, "Please tell your story. Someone I know is being stalked, and it might help her." I looked around the dinner table. In the distance my friend Bryan Busby, who's a local weatherman, was putting dollar bills into the outfit of the restaurant's belly dancer. Amidst all that excitement, one of the people at our table for 22 was reaching out. The card was unsigned. But I learned the person who was being stalked was in a group I spoke to at a women's center a few weeks later.

My 30th birthday present to myself was reaching out to help others. And telling my story in small groups of victims of all sorts of crimes was a way to do that. My pledge was to do it for one year. I haven't stopped yet. By helping others understand how fear destroys us, I began to shake off its effects in my life.

I talked about fear being an acronym, F-E-A-R, which stands for False Evidence Appearing Real. I told crime victims that giving in to fear is like having a virus that eventually will take over its host. And I told them sometimes you have to do things even when you're filled with fear.

An example of this was the first dating relationship I had after the trial. And, finally, I shared in my talks the idea of fighting fear with words of good report. Whenever I felt haunted by my past as a stalking victim, I'd find something good that happened to me during the trauma and talk about that. For example, along the painful journey of being stalked, I had been promoted to anchor the evening news, covered a host of high-profile stories, attended Hall of Famer George Brett's final baseball game. I even attended Brett's pre-game luncheon at the stadium where I was seated with Brett's friend Rush Limbaugh. Believe it or not, Limbaugh never talked politics. I'd gone to the superbowl in Miami and watched the announcement that my friend Kellen Winslow would be inducted into the NFL Hall of Fame. The parties in

Miami were legendary. We shared a limousine with Kellen's cousin, Michael Winslow, the actor who does the wacky sounds in the *Police Academy* movies. My life was charmed at a time when the stalker was ruthless.

I continue to shake the shadow of fear by remembering good times come with the bad. That's God's blessing. And all things end. That's God's plan.

THE KANSAS CITY STAR.

ember 26, 1995   METROPOLITAN EDITION ★★ $1.50

Fleeing a stalker's shadow

**Channel 4's Harris Faulkner
knew terror for 18 months.**

By STEVE PENN
Staff Writer

For 18 months in 1993 and 1994, Harris Faulkner lived in fear.

Viewers of WDAF-TV, Channel 4, could see only a composed professional delivering the news. Not the woman with such inner turmoil. Not the woman who lived behind double-locked doors. Not the woman who had an escort home almost every night. All because a man she'd dated was stalking her.

"It was just a campaign of terror," Faulkner said in a recent interview. "Over time, you tire.

But he never seemed to lose his desire to do this. He just kept getting stronger."

Court orders couldn't stop him. Locks and a private security guard couldn't slow him. Eventually, his persistence forced her to move from her Quality Hill apartment to a house south of the Country Club Plaza.

She spent her entire savings — she won't say how much — for a security guard to watch her house and follow her whenever she left. She even considered ending her television news career.

"When police tell you to take things seriously, that wakes you up," Faulkner said. "I knew I was starting to always feel frightened. I knew I was becoming very wary of my surroundings."

According to court records reviewed by *The*

Kansas City Star, her stalker ultimately was convicted and is getting counseling out of state.

Faulkner agreed to share her story only if he was not named. Identifying him — a former colleague her age who worked off-camera — would only glorify his actions, she believes. She decided to publicize her ordeal after she researched stalking for a recent news story aired on Channel 4.

"When we had the entire story together, it touched me in such a way that it made me want to share with people the fact that this has happened to me," Faulkner said.

Letting people understand what she went through — and that stalking victims can do

See **NEW, A-26,** Col. 1

Harris Faulkner
... headlines became reality

A-26   The Kansas City Star   Sunday, November 26, 1995

New phone number, locks fail to discourage stalker

Continued from A-1

things to protect themselves — might prevent someone else from being stalked, she believes.

She began her tale smiling and confident — almost as if she were delivering the news. But her poise periodically dissolved as she tearfully recounted the almost daily barrage of intrusions into her life. When the ordeal began, Jackson

If you are being stalked, you should:

■ Call the Metropolitan Organization to Counter Sexual Assault at **931-4527** or the 24-hour crisis hot line at **531-0233.**

■ Install a telephone caller identification device.

■ Document all instances of harassment or stalking.

■ Seek legal assistance or ask a court to issue a restraining

---

IN THE CIRCUIT COURT OF JACKSON COUNTY, MISSOURI
☒ AT KANSAS CITY   ☐ AT INDEPENDENCE

Harris K. Faulkner
_____
PETITIONER

NO._____ DR93-4808

VS.

▬▬▬▬▬▬▬▬▬▬▬
RESPONDENT

D/O/B __12/27/65__   **Black Male**

S.S. # ▬▬▬▬▬▬▬▬

(court stamp)

FULL ORDER OF PROTECTION
ADULT ABUSE

---

7) Court costs are assessed against _____ Petitioner _____ Respondent _____ Other _____

FAILURE TO OBSERVE THE TERMS OF THIS ORDER MAY RESULT IN PROSECUTION FOR COMMISSION OF A CLASS A MISDEMEANOR, WITH A MAXIMUM PUNISHMENT OF ONE YEAR IMPRISONMENT, $1,000.00 FINE OR BOTH, OR A CLASS D FELONY, WITH A MAXIMUM PUNISHMENT OF FIVE YEARS IMPRISONMENT, $5000.00 FINE OR BOTH. SEE §558 R.S. Mo. and §560 R.S. Mo.

This Full Order of Protection is effective for ____180____ days unless sooner terminated or extended by this Court.

__May 26, 1993__
_____
DATE

_____
JUDGE

EXPIRATION DATE: ___11/22/93___ _____ 11:59:59 P.M.

THE RESPONDENT WAS SERVED A COPY OF THIS ORDER ON_____ BY_____

DEPUTY COURT ADMINISTRATOR.

CIRCT 1431 - 4/89

THERE ARE IMPORTANT ADDITIONAL INSTRUCTIONS
AND INFORMATION ON REVERSE SIDE.

Harris with co-anchor Phil Witt (on left) and weatherman Mike Thompson (on right). Billboards 1994.

Harris with Bryant Gumbel at his golf tournament, March 1995, Orlando, Florida

Harris with actress Shirley MacLaine, Unity Temple on the Plaza, February 1994

(Left) Harris' 30th Birthday Bash with friend Polly Taylor, October 1995

(Right) Harris with friend Kellen Winslow, Arrowhead Stadium Club, 1994

Harris with close friend Ed Crony, Stockton Lake, 1996

Harris with co-anchor Phil Witt and game show host Bob Eubanks (on left), Hollywood Squares Night, 1994

(Left) Harris emcees Blacks in Government Gala during happier times, one year after stalking trial ends, 1996

Harris making Magic Johnson laugh, interview, May 1998

Harris with friend Nick Lowery, February 1999

Harris with Tae Bo King, Billy Blanks, after tough workout, Bartle Hall, April 1999

Harris with Bob Costas (on right) and Bob Uecker (left), Charity event, February 1999

CHAPTER THREE

Why Bad Things Happen

In third grade, Mrs. Crawley told us to pay attention or we would suffer the consequences.

WHEN I WAS being stalked, I was often angry with God. It was difficult for me to comprehend how He could let bad things happen. God showed me that while He loves us, He allows us to experience a mixture of good and bad to help us grow. Flowers are a good example of this. It takes both sunshine and rain to make them grow. Sometimes it may seem like it's raining non-stop, but only God knows the right mix for you. And you may be able to learn from the rain that's falling in someone else's life.

* * * * *

In the spring of 1992, I had my first experience with breaking news behind the anchor desk. I always thought the anchors got to see a story before reading it on the air. But not this time.

"Harris, real quick. You're reading this. It's in the TelePrompTer. There's no time to get hard copy to you. Just read the words you see on the screen in front of you. It's a child abuse story —" the producer said quickly. He was talking to me through my earpiece.

Suddenly, the newscast music faded in and out and my microphone was open. The camera was on me.

"We have some breaking news out of Leavenworth, Kansas, tonight. Police tell us they were called to a home where seven children live. There was a report that one of those children was missing. Tonight, police say they've found the body of four-year-old Stephen Brown. They say the child apparently had died days before and someone put his tiny body in a large trash bag, filling it up with some kind of cement.

"Police found the cement block hardened around the child's body, left on the back porch of the home," I said. My voice was beginning to quiver. I couldn't control it. A tear began rolling from my left eye. Then, a tear from my right eye. I continued, "Police have taken the child's mother into custody. We don't know how the four-year-old died or the condition or whereabouts of the other children at this hour. We have a news crew at the scene, and we'll continue to update this story as we learn more."

I lifted my right hand to wipe away a tear. Now the camera was on a shot of Phil and me. Phil looked concerned, somewhat surprised that I was crying. Right on the air he asked, "Are you okay?"

"Yes, that story just got me right here." I pointed to my heart. "It just breaks my heart."

"Yes, I know," Phil said softly. And he smoothly moved onto the next story in the newscast.

* * * * *

The Lord must be very busy trying to get our attention. I believe when awful things happen they involve more than the people who suffer or the people who commit the wrongdoing. Sometimes bad things happen to get our attention.

For days after we reported that child abuse case, I labored over it. It was my last thought before I fell asleep and my first thought in the morning. I prayed that little Stephen Brown was in a better place. And I prayed for the rest of us.

We should be concerned about the evil that dwells among us. In fact, it's our responsibility to deal with it.

For me, the lesson was to take a closer look at how the media handle stories that really matter — like a child suffering. It was suddenly very clear that reporters are more likely to chase celebrities, athletes and politicians around like the world is ending than they are to press for the truth in the advocacy of a child. That's hard for me as a journalist to admit. Through years of watching celebrities suck up society's focus more than defenseless people in trouble, fighting for more of a balance in news coverage has become a goal of mine. The lesson of that one story years ago left a lasting impression on me. Who knows what others may have experienced through watching our broadcast that night, but I'm convinced it got a lot of people's attention. Everyone learns in different ways, though. So I imagine there are things happening all the time that teach lessons to each of us based upon what God's plan is for us at the moment. What will it take for God to get *your* attention?

* * * * *

God doesn't cause bad things to happen, but he may allow them to occur. Maybe He doesn't remove us from harm's way or perhaps He doesn't spare a loved one from losing a job or He lets it rain for so many days that families are flooded out of their homes. You may recognize these scenarios as pain you've experienced. We live in a dangerous world, and sometimes there are accidents or random acts of violence. Why doesn't God protect us? Questioning God may prove to be less helpful than looking for His plan — a plan which always comes with blessings. There is a blessing in every bad thing that happens. We just have to work through the pain to find it. For me, turning my stalking nightmare into a way to help other victims cope has been a silver lining. In a later chapter, you'll read about how to uncover His plan for your life.

For now, keep the following in mind, which works best when you repeat these words before each reason ... **BAD THINGS HAPPEN BECAUSE:**

• **God wants to get our attention.** God is teaching us something about ourselves. He may be trying to get us to stop repeating mistakes.

• **God wants to feel needed.** He wants us to lean on and trust in Him.

• **We complain.** We forget to be thankful for what we have and the people in our lives who love us.

• **We try to force life to be what we want.** We attempt to make things happen our way rather than going with the flow

God has put into place. We literally go against His will. This happens a lot when relationships go bad. Maybe you've been in love with someone who strays or just falls out of love. You may try to win that person back, and in the process end up doing some silly or even hurtful things.

• **The devil is at work.** There is evil on earth, and its disciples are among us. Not to sound too paranoid, but you may have come across those people who just seem to take pleasure in doing wrong. The devil, to me, is more of a spirit of hatefulness or meanness that dwells in our neighbors, than it is the icon with pointed ears and a pitchfork. No, the devil is not *one* being, it's many. In fact, sometimes that evil spirit can dwell in us. When we feel sorry for ourselves, we want to punish whoever is hurting us. You've heard the saying, "Revenge is not ours." There were never truer words spoken. When someone does you wrong, let God handle it. Evil energy only thrives when we get in on the wrongdoing.

• **We're being tested.** God sometimes tests us to see if we'll continue doing right, even when it's not easy. This was a tough one for me to grasp. It isn't easy being sweet under pressure! But I've learned that doing the right thing — when I want to and when I don't — is God's plan.

CHAPTER FOUR

God Sends Us Teachers

"The best reporter lets the people affected tell the story. They are the teachers, and the reporter is the blackboard. Listen and be still so the teachers can write."

— Scott Libin, Former Director
Poynter Institute for Media Studies

DO YOU EVER WONDER why this or that person is in your life? Maybe there's a neighbor who just bugs you by being so nice. You know the kind. She bakes cookies for all the newcomers in the neighborhood. She volunteers at all the parent-child events at your kid's school. She even offers to watch your kids so you can have a break. She just plain makes you look bad, because she's such a darn good person. My response to these do-gooders, "Yikes!" And that's exactly why God keeps putting these people in my life. They are a reminder that He not only wants us to care about the world, but to *take care of* our neighbors. I tend to get caught up in the worldly issues that are huge to tackle. I end up doing little to solve them.

For example, one of my interests is in world literacy. That's a big job. A year ago, I set out to research all the literacy groups in the United States. A search of the Internet turned up thousands of choices. I ended up giving about $100 to some place in New Mexico.

The very next week, I was standing in line at the grocery store in my neighborhood. This woman behind me was so nice.

"Hi, aren't you that woman on TV?" she asked.

"Yes, I'm flattered that you watch. I'm on Channel 4," I responded.

"I thought so. Where were you last weekend?" she asked.

"Oh, here and there," I returned. I thought, what an odd question.

"Well, you missed it. A great read-a-thon to raise money for Kansas City libraries. I read 15 books to dozens of kids," she bragged.

"Oh, the good we were doing that day, your TV station covered it. You should have been there. I mean, since you read the news and all. But I'm sure with your busy schedule you were just over-committed or something. Maybe next year we'll see you there," she added in such a sweet voice.

Yuck! This woman was getting annoying. First, she pointed out the obvious. Yes, I was a bubble-head for not knowing about the read-a-thon. But then she forgave me. I'm sorry, but her great attitude and sweet disposition were killing me.

You see, while I was scouring the nation for literacy programs, I could have lent my voice and time to my own community. I didn't even look there. I'm sure my money was helping someone learn to read in New Mexico, but if I'd researched closer to home … well, you know the rest. God put that grocery store lady in my path to remind me to take care of the people nearest me to the best of my ability. He wants me — all of us — to look out for our neighbors. Then, and only then, will the world take care of itself. That woman was a teacher sent by God.

Some of you may refer to God's teachers as angels. I've had some experiences with teachers who brought about tough lessons. Some were relationships that didn't work out or friendships that revealed areas in me that needed work. Every one of these people has a lesson for us. I believe we must first recognize that, and then pay attention. That way we won't have to keep learning the same lessons over and over.

* * * * *

"I have fights with God. I want to know why those 19 little children had to die. I want to know why!" Jannie Coverdale said. She didn't shed a tear.

Mrs. Coverdale told me she was all cried out for that day. But she said she'd cry the next day and every day after that for the rest of her life.

Mrs. Coverdale worked near the Alfred P. Murrah Federal Building in downtown Oklahoma City. Her grandchildren, four-year-old Elijah and two-year-old Aaron, were her whole world. And they were her responsibility. Her son and daughter-in-law had been going through rough times. So Mrs. Coverdale offered to take the two little boys and give them some stability.

Each morning before work, she dropped Elijah and Aaron off at the daycare center on the second floor of the Federal Building. Then she would leave to go to her office in another government building down the street.

On Wednesday, April 19, 1995, she was running late. She didn't feel well that morning, but she went through the routine anyway. After leaving the boys at the daycare center, Mrs. Coverdale left the building. Moments later, at 9:02 in the morning, the Federal Building exploded.

"Why wasn't I with them? Why didn't I die instead of them?" she asked. Her face was puffed up with pain.

"Harris, every reporter asks me to tell my story, but it's not a story to me. It's a dream, and God's going to let me wake up. I just know it," Mrs. Coverdale continued.

Her eyes peered into mine. I could almost feel her pain. Something hurt me deeply. Maybe it was that I understood her anger with God. It was now one year after the bombing, and God hadn't healed her one bit. How cruel, I thought. And then this ...

"You told me before that your family's been mainly leaning on you through all of this. What do you tell them?" I asked.

"I tell them not to lose their faith," she answered quickly.

"But you said —" I was cut short by her.

"I know I said I'm angry with God. But don't misunderstand. He created us — all of us. Even that monster who took our loved ones away last year. But I still believe God is here with us. And he has a mission for me now, a plan. I seldom sleep anymore. I have all this energy now. And I spend it telling the world — everyone I meet — to be kinder to one another," she said. Now the tears were flowing.

I was wrong. God had begun to heal her, but she had lessons to learn and to teach along the way. I was in her path.

When we hugged each other good-bye, Mrs. Coverdale whispered something in my ear. The photographer who had shot our interview was putting away the gear, and I don't know if he heard her. But I'll never forget what she said.

"Don't ever lose your faith. God tests us. And some of us, like me, live to tell his message," Mrs. Coverdale said softly.

The photographer and I were in Oklahoma City for just a couple of days gathering stories on the one-year anniversary of the bombing that killed 168 people. I believe those who lived to tell their stories are some of God's greatest teachers. Although I have never seen Mrs. Coverdale again, her words and her un-shakable strength are always with me, in spirit.

* * * * *

Sometimes we are the teachers — being shaped and readied by our tough times and painful experiences. Maybe it's in our survival that others can learn. Perhaps it's a hopeful attitude we exude while suffering. Or maybe it's the way we stay strong in our faith that is a lesson to those around us. I believe we must be careful to do what we preach, especially in times of strife. When there's trouble of any kind, it seems like my friends and col-leagues often look to me for answers. And my answer is always the same: Don't give up and be kind to those around you. If it's a tornado, a car accident, a stressful situation at work — no matter what.

For some people the only evidence that there is a God might be what they see in us. Are you prepared to be the light they see? If you say yes, then you're one of God's teachers. And in this we can all be His teachers. We can be the evidence they can see and touch that proves He is real.

The following are some of the teachers God has sent me. The list could grow every day. I think our parents are our original teachers. My parents, Bob and Shirley, gave me the basics. They taught me to treat people the way I want to be treated and about the value of humility before God and others.

"Raising a child is the most important work you'll ever do."
— **Bobby Harris,** *my dad*

"I lost an eye, and the scars on my body are still healing. But my heart is intact. I can love my husband and my children. And I can feel their love. And isn't that the meaning of life."
— **Ruth Heald,** Oklahoma City bombing survivor

"Life is just this way. Someone will always be there standing in the way of your dream. You have to think them out of the way."
— **Shirley MacLaine,** actress (see photo)

"Our business is competitive. So is just about everything else in life. You decide how long you want to hang in there, and don't blame anyone else if you give up."
— **Bryant Gumbel,** network anchor, CBS (see photo)

"Eat a little of everything on your plate. Variety keeps us from getting bored."
— **Shirley Harris,** my mom

"Pick your battles carefully. But definitely stand for something and fight for it when you must."
— **Phil Witt,** anchor, WDAF-TV 4 (see photo)

"Be a student of the game. Whatever your game is, know it better than anybody."
—**Kellen Winslow,** NFL Hall of Famer/ESPN commentator (see photo)

"Too much of one thing — no matter if it's good or bad — is just too much."
—**Jana Blackburn-Calkins,** producer, WDAF-TV 4

"Don't run from what hurts you. Deal with life where you are."
— **Michael Delorenzo,** actor, "New York Undercover"

"Marry for love and stick it out. And marry a younger man. We outlive them, you know. It's no fun growing old alone."
— **Queen Temple,** my 87-year-old grandmother

"I do what I do for love — to give and receive love. It's worth more than money. It's more beautiful than the most fit body. Love is the thing."

— Billy Blanks, *Tae-Bo creator (see photo)*

CHAPTER FIVE

Getting Unstuck

"If you fall out of the boat, don't stand up. Your feet will get caught in the rocks below and you'll be swept under by the current. If you're stuck, you die. So relax and lean into the water facing upstream. It's courage, not might, that will keep you from getting stuck."

—Chris, Rafting Guide
Colorado River, September 1997

WE ALL GET STUCK ... caught in a rut, at some point in life. Sometimes it's our circumstances, such as working at a dead-end job or having a spouse who loses a job and the financial stresses that can follow. Perhaps it's something in us, like a lack of energy or drive, boredom or low self-esteem. Whatever the contributing factors, getting in a rut, for most of us, is inevitable. If we want to find personal success — that's code for happiness — getting out of a rut must also be inevitable.

First, how do you know if you're stuck? Answer the following questions "yes" or "no."

(1) Do you look forward to getting out of bed tomorrow morning?
(2) Are you able to leave work behind and find happiness at home?
(3) Are you at peace with your co-workers, family members or people you spend the most time with every day?
(4) Are you striving toward a goal/dream or living it?
(5) Would people around you say you're an optimistic and positive person?

If you said "no" to four or more of the above, you are CHRONICALLY STUCK. But don't panic. It happens to the best of us.

* * * * *

"Accidents happen. But what happened here today was no accident. Greenville police tell us a man carrying a sawed-off shotgun walked into that building over there. They say he made his way to an office on the second floor, shattered the glass door with the butt of the gun, staggered into the office and opened fire. Witnesses say the man reloaded the gun, again and again.

"Tonight, one person is dead and two others injured. And

police have arrested a suspect.

"Earlier, our cameras were rolling when the gunman poked his gun out of one of the second floor office windows, apparently aiming down at police officers. As you can see in this video, there were people on the sidewalks walking to and from nearby buildings. You see that they're trying to take cover. Fortunately, no gunfire was exchanged at that point.

"We're told the suspect is in the city jail waiting to be formally charged by prosecutors. Reporting live from the scene, I'm Harris Faulkner. Allan, back to you in the studio."

"Not bad for the kid's first live shot," the cameraman, Kevin O'Brien, said smiling.

"I was pretty nervous. Could you tell?" I asked.

"Well, only after I figured out what that tapping noise was in the background," he laughed.

I had been so scared, my legs were shaking uncontrollably, making the heels of my pumps click against the pavement. You could hear the tap, tap, tap coming from my feet. It must have looked ridiculous to the reporters who were doing live reports near me. But none of that mattered. My first live report was over.

* * * * *

As the news van pulled into the parking lot of the television station, I felt a strange sensation. It wasn't a chill exactly, but my arms were covered with goosebumps. I crossed my arms to rub them with my hands to get rid of the goosebumps.

"You ah-right there, kid?" Kevin asked.

"I just got a weird feeling," I answered. I thought to myself, this is it — this is what I'm supposed to be doing — it's coming so naturally to me, because it's part of God's plan. "It's probably nothing," I said, staring out of the passenger-side window.

"Well, here we are. Over the two-way I heard the assignment editor say she wanted a wrap-up of the day's events at the scene, for the ten o'clock news tonight. If you hurry up and write it, I'll edit the video," Kevin offered. What a nice guy. He was so patient. He reminded me of Santa Claus, or at least how Santa would look in the off-season. Kevin had a round face, rosy cheeks and a gray beard that was almost white in some spots. His stomach was full. He looked jolly.

* * * * *

"Well, looky here. If it isn't the new reporter," the news director, Roy Hardee, exclaimed. He seemed to like teasing me. Roy shook my hand and told me how well I'd done in the field on my first day.

"We spanked the competition. Got there first, and we're the only one to get video of police arresting the suspect!" Roy patted Kevin on the back.

In the center of the room, a young woman sat at a large desk. She was trying to answer all the calls coming in.

"Hey, can I get some help? Somebody pick up one of these lines!" she demanded. Carolyn Cusbit ran the Assignment Desk. She had a lot of influence in the newsroom because she dispatched all of the reporters and photographers and decided who covered which stories. She was tough, but fair. She could be bitingly sarcastic — not offensive, just brutally honest.

"Hold it down. I'm trying to hear. It's the police department on the line," Carolyn said. We turned to watch her. No one talked.

"He'll talk on camera? And we can get into the jail with our cameras? Okay. In the pink suit? Oh, yeah, I gotcha. Tomorrow morning at nine. Thanks." Carolyn hung up the receiver and motioned for me to come over to her desk.

"It's not the ensemble I would have chosen, but that little outfit your mom must have picked out got the suspect's attention. He says he'll only talk to the woman in pink he saw flitting about the scene. Anyway, miss thang, you got yourself an exclusive with the alleged gunman," she said in her brassy voice. Soon, I learned she only talked that way to people she liked and respected. Lucky me.

* * * * *

My home for two weeks while I looked for an apartment was a small, musty motel room. I kicked off my shoes and changed into my bathrobe. I grabbed a pen and my journal and collapsed into an old, cracking, but soft leather chair.

October 23, 1990

Wow! What a first day! The news director came and picked me up this morning at 8:30. When we got to the station, he took me to human resources to get payroll and health insurance forms. I was in the newsroom filling out those forms when Carolyn began screaming into the building's intercom system. She was looking for a reporter to go to the scene of a multiple shooting. After a few minutes, she looked over at me and said I was her last resort.

This was the most memorable day in my 25 years on earth. And tomorrow I'll get the exclusive interview with the shooter. I just wish Mom and Dad could have seen me today.

It's hard to believe that just ten months ago, I was in Los Angeles dreaming about holding a microphone and talking to thousands of people. I was stuck in a job and place I didn't want to be. Only God could have given me the courage to get unstuck.

* * * * *

On a cloudy day in January of 1990, my girlfriend Liz Warren and I were walking our usual Sunday 10-mile loop through the Hollywood Hills.

"Can you see it from here?" I asked.

"What?" Liz returned.

"The sign — you know, the sign," I said, out of breath. Our pace was fast and non-stop.

"What is it with you and the Hollywood sign? No one actually goes up there except maybe somebody who's wasted or drunk," Liz said.

"I know it's a haul, but let's get off this paved path and do it — go to the top," I pleaded.

"We've already been at this for over an hour. Next Sunday, okay. Next Sunday. We both have to work early tomorrow morning. I'll be too sore to even think if we do it today," Liz reasoned.

"Yeah. Work. In early to help reorganize and catalog decades of old writings. Sounds titillating," I complained.

"Hey, I'm glad to get the distraction. You're the accounting manager — doing the books, payroll and everything. At least you don't have time to get bored. All I do is answer the phones," Liz said between heavy breaths.

"Why do you fret so?" she asked.

Liz had a thick English accent. It made everything she said sound important. She'd come from London to Los Angeles a few months earlier. Liz was tall and thin. Her face was strong with a prominent chin. She had very short blond hair. She wasn't beautiful, but striking — a face you'd never forget. Liz wanted to work behind the scenes in Hollywood, eventually producing or directing big studio films. Paramount was her favorite studio. I believed she could do it. But she was so realistic. She plotted a slow course, networking at some key events she got invited to, through the literary agency where we worked. Her plan was okay, I guess. She definitely had something I lacked — patience. Maybe her age made a difference. I was 23. She was nearly 14 years older.

* * * * *

Liz raised her arm in the air and snapped her fingers and asked, "Hey, are you still with me? You've been awfully quiet the last mile or so."

"Oh, sorry. I guess I was thinking about what I really want to do," I answered.

"TV reporting," Liz remarked, stone-faced.

"Yeah. Don't say it with such disdain. You know I've been doing an internship at that public access station for a few weeks now," I said.

"Internship — the fancy American word for working for free," Liz quipped.

We laughed. And I said soberly, "I'm learning a lot. All the technical stuff and even how to put stories together."

"Then what?" Liz asked.

"Well, I have a chance to do another internship. This time at a real TV station — Channel 13. You know it's tough to get these opportunities after college. I mean, I don't get credit or anything," I said.

"Let me get this straight — you're already working a day job at the agency and most weekend mornings at that public access station. When do you have time for another —" Liz stopped talking and shook her head.

"What?"

"When are you going to sleep? You're killing yourself and why? Harris, people don't go from accounting to TV news," Liz said, matter-of-factly.

"Liz, I'm stuck. I've been in some form of accounting job since I graduated college almost three years ago. And I'm not happy. I thought I wanted to be an accountant. Now, I know it's TV news. And I'd rather get no sleep working toward something than lose sleep wondering what if."

"And *what if* you do the two internships and nothing happens? How are you so sure it's the right thing to do?"

"You wouldn't believe me if I told you."

"Try me," Liz challenged.

Liz didn't believe me, but she listened. I told her I had had a conversation with God asking for answers or direction. I had always been the type of person who loved with all my heart whatever I pursued. It was that intense love that kept me dedicated and focused. But now the love for any one thing was gone. I was stuck.

* * * * *

Pulling up to the Channel 13 guard gate in a silver hatchback Ford. I was nervous and excited.

"Harris Faulkner. I'm here to begin my newsroom internship," I told the security guard.

"Ah, yes. I have you on my list for today," the guard said without looking up from a clipboard he apparently was using to check in visitors.

"Harris, huh. I expected a man. Odd name you got there," he said.

"Yeah, my parents wanted a boy," I joked.

He finally looked at me. "Well, they didn't get that. Not even close," the guard said, trying to get a closer look at me by leaning out of his little shack. Was this old guy flirting with me? My hands were shaking as I pulled into the parking spot that the guard was pointing out. I checked myself out in the rearview mirror. My curly brown hair was a little tamer than usual. I powdered my face, to keep it from looking oily. I so seldom wore make-up that my face itched a bit, but overall I was presentable. I had on a bright orange suit. The matching high heels were killing my feet. But no complaints. I was about to walk into a real television station with real journalists putting on news for the second largest city in the nation. Oh, I must be nuts, I thought. What will they think of me?

* * * * *

Walking into the newsroom, I heard a sound that would change me forever, and it would be a part of my life for years to come. It was the rattle and hum of phones ringing and computer keyboards clicking beneath busy, furious hands. It was the sound of a newsroom drilling toward the next deadline — a one-hour evening newscast with breaking news on fires, crimes and stories about children escaping the gangster life. Certain voices were heard above the rest.

"Yeah, man, I just wanna double check. You say the kid, the black kid, had a gun. Oh, it wasn't a gun. But he's dead — right? The cops, they..." a reporter debriefed a source for a story that was dividing the city along white and black lines.

Another reporter, Dana James, gathered facts for a report one of the anchors would read, "Do you know what started the fire yet? Uh-huh. And the woman who was burned, is she — okay, I just want to verify a couple more points."

After listening for a few minutes, just standing motionless, someone came up and tapped me on the shoulder. He was a nice man who walked me over to an area where there was a huge desk with a lot of telephones. The curved desk was raised off the floor a few inches. From behind the desk, you could see the entire newsroom. The man called it the Assignment Desk. He left me there. Another nice guy stood up and extended his hand.

"Well, hey. I'm Bill Pratt, and you must be Harris," he said, shaking my hand. Bill looked like a dad. He had on a dress shirt and tie under a cardigan sweater. He peered over his glasses to look at me.

"Hello, yes, I'm Harris Faulkner. I'm here for the internship program," I said.

"I'm kind of the coordinator for this group. Although you all look like you can handle yourselves just fine. Harris, have a seat and fill out this form," Bill said.

There was another young woman and two young men sitting in chairs, forming a half-circle around Bill. They were the other interns. The young woman had just graduated college, and the two guys were still in school. Clearly, they were younger than I. Maybe that's what Bill saw, too. He eventually gave me more responsibility than the others. But we all started out the same way — making fresh coffee for the newsroom and answering phones on the Assignment Desk. Bill took us on a tour of the station. My favorite part was the studio, where the anchors delivered the evening news. I wondered what it would be like to sit in their seats behind the beautiful glass and wood desk and talk to hundreds of thousands of people each night. The other interns remarked how much it looked like a movie set with bright lights and how everything was on wheels. Even the walls were movable.

A man walked through the studio past us. He was in a great hurry. He looked important — he wore a shirt and tie with the shirtsleeves rolled up just under his elbows. He seemed to barely notice us.

"Who's that?" I asked.

"That's Jeff Wald, the news director. The big cheese — the man with the power to make or break a news anchor's career," Bill said, only half-jokingly.

"He's a busy guy, so we want to make sure we stay out of his way. Got it, guys?" Bill continued.

The other interns chimed in, in agreement. I, on the other hand, wanted to meet that fast-walking, powerful man. But that wouldn't happen for some time.

* * * * *

One month into it, the schedule was tearing me down. Maybe Liz was right. Was it worth all the physical torture? I thought so. But I needed help. My parents had taught me to pray when I was in trouble. Surely God would think my situation was minor. I prayed anyway, asking for strength. God answered my prayer with more strength than I'd ever dreamed.

I woke up each morning at dawn, ran a few miles, stretched out and dressed for work. Then I put in eight hours at the literary agency, and I worked from five to midnight at Channel 13. On weekends, I worked at the public access cable station from six in the morning until noon, learning the technical side of broadcasting, such as using the videotape machines to edit stories together. I had the strength I needed to get it all done well.

Then I prayed for courage. Again, my prayer was answered. When I thought I couldn't do any more, I became courageous in my pursuit by joining a small theater group. Sunday nights we'd work on projecting our voices and breathing evenly when delivering lines of dialogue. I was scared to death to be in front of an audience, even if it was just a dozen or so actors. But God had given me the courage to do it.

* * * * *

By late spring, I'd been at Channel 13 for three months. I was going out on stories with reporters. My mentor was an African-American journalist named Brian Jenkins. He always got the facts right, and his interview style put people at ease. I tried to observe him at work as often as possible. Brian said he was impressed by my work ethic.

At the station, I usually milled about watching the newscasts take shape from reporters' notebooks to the finished product of their voices under pictures on videotape. I was doing just that when Bill caught up with me.

"Hey, Harris. We've got a situation, and it means everyone, even the interns, have to do more than their share. You're now my assistant on the Assignment Desk. That means I may need you to set up interviews for reporters. You may have to drive a news van to a scene to shuttle tapes or information back and forth," Bill spoke deliberately. It was as if he didn't want to have to repeat himself.

"Sure, Bill. May I ask what's going on?" I responded.

"Yeah, kid. It's the Middle East — the beginning of something they're calling Desert Shield. There are some of us (Americans) over there. And there is some stuff about American civilians leaving that area immediately. In fact, we've confirmed at least two people from L.A. are there. Most of our resources are focused on that right now. That's why I need your help," Bill said.

I immediately went to work, organizing the Assignment Desk, filing away some things. wiping down the desktop and phones with Formula 409 cleaner. Being an accountant had taught me the importance of an orderly workspace. Brian Jenkins walked by.

"Wow, are we expecting a Presidential visit?" Brian asked.

"Hey, Brian. Nah, I just wanted to get the place together. How did your story on the homeless woman turnout?" I returned.

"I guess that depends on how you look at it. I mean, we got some great stuff from her. But she's still homeless," Brian said, thoughtfully.

"Yeah, good point," I said.

"By the way, thanks for setting up that interview with the

teenage dad at the mission. His volunteer work is amazing," Brian said.

"Sure, I wish I could have been there," I said.

"Yeah. They've got you desk-side. The Mid-East thing?" Brian asked.

"Yep. I got a new title — Desk Assistant. And I'll be making five bucks an hour now," I said proudly.

"It's a start. Between here and the public access station, you'll learn how to do just about everything," Brian said.

"Everything but actually be on TV," I returned.

"You ought to check out the NABJ Convention. It's here this year. I think they're holding in on the west side," Brian suggested.

"NA — what?" I asked.

"The National Association of Black Journalist Convention. It's got workshops. Great guest speakers, like Oprah Winfrey and Ed Bradley. But basically the whole thing's just a giant job fair," Brian answered.

"Sounds expensive," I said.

"It's worth it though. Hey, I'd better get this story written. Then I'm outta here," Brian smiled.

"Thanks for the info," I said.

"Any time, kid. You have a good weekend," Brian said. He thought of something else as he walked away, "The convention's next Thursday through the weekend.

"See ya Monday," he said.

* * * * *

Sunday night and still no way for me to go to that journalism convention. Walking along the Santa Monica pier, I listened to the waves coming in and going out. They were like God breathing evenly, endlessly. I sat down on the sand a few feet from the water's edge.

Looking into the blackened waters to a horizon lit up by a bright moon, I thanked God for the strength and courage He'd given me to accomplish all the work I was doing. And I thanked

Him for putting talented and generous people in my path, like Bill Pratt, Brian Jenkins and many others. I didn't have the money or a way to get the time off from the literary agency, but I wanted to go to that journalist convention and job fair. I asked God to please help me find a way.

* * * * *

"Monday morning and you're late. Good sign," Liz said teasingly.

"I slept in. I never do that. I don't know what came over me," I explained.

"Oh, sure. Sleeping in. Is that what we're calling it now!" Liz teased.

"Did your hot date Saturday night turn into a steamy weekend fling?" she continued boldly.

"No way. I mean, he's a babe, but, well, ya know," I responded.

"Yeah. Whoever heard of having an *entire* wonderful weekend with a great guy. Not the die-hard workaholic, Harris Kimberley Faulkner. I just thought you might have had some fun. Call me crazy," Liz said sarcastically.

"Okay, crazy," I quipped.

"You'll like this. I'm typing an announcement. The Swansons are closing this place for a couple of days," Liz said.

"Why?" I asked.

"Something about new carpets and remodeling. It's this Thursday and Friday," Liz answered.

"Cool!" I said, grinning.

As I sat down at my desk, I went over what just happened in my head. I couldn't believe it. There was now a way for me to get the time off from the agency to go to the NABJ Convention.

It was a busy afternoon. The time just seemed to fly by. Driving into Channel 13's parking lot, the old guard waved me through the security gate. He was on the phone. He was a nice man. We'd been introduced. He was Thomas Stewart. He'd lived in East L.A. his whole life. He was a grandfather now, and his wife had died some years earlier.

By the time I got out of my car, he was off the phone and walking over to me. Brian Jenkins was parking his car a couple of spaces away.

"The nightshift's rollin' in. You doin' all right, Ms. Faulkner? You sure do look good today," the guard said playfully.

"Well, thank you, Mr. Stewart. I'm doing just peachy," I said. Brian walked over to us.

"Just Peachy. Faulkner, you're such a trip," Brian said.

"Are you making fun of me?" I asked.

"No one talks like that. You're an original, I'll give you that," Brian teased.

"She's the real deal. When are you TV types gonna put her on the tube?" Mr. Stewart asked.

"Oh, I'm a long way from working on TV in Los Angeles, Mr. Stewart. But thanks for the vote of confidence," I responded.

"All right, then where? I'm tellin' you, I have an eye for these things. I do. I've seen 'em come and go here, and you could do it," Mr. Stewart said.

"You're sweet. I'm working on it. Speaking of work," I said.

"Yeah, let's head in," Brian said.

We exchanged good-byes with the guard.

As we entered the newsroom, a photographer walked up to us.

"Brian, we've got a problem with that video we shot last week," the photographer said softly.

"Okay, let me put my things down at my desk and I'll meet you in the editing booth. Harris, check ya later," Brian said, scrambling off.

On my way to the Assignment Desk, I noticed the newsroom coffee pot was nearly empty. I put my purse down and said hello to Bill and the interns, and went over to the coffee machine.

"Hey, you trying to kill us?" Ross Becker asked. He was one of the evening anchors. A gorgeous, tall blond with a great voice.

"What are you talking about? You don't like my coffee?" I asked.

"Oh, honey, it's not a matter of like. There are safety and health concerns here!" Ross laughed and walked on.

That was odd. Bill and the others were laughing hysterically.

"I keep saying, Harris, it's not your technique. It's the machine," Bill said, holding back more laughter.

"Yeah, Harris, we all have our talents and, well, our weaknesses, too," one of the interns quipped.

"So when were you guys going to tell me?" I asked.

They all just laughed. I didn't drink the stuff, but I had noticed that sometimes after making a fresh pot, the coffee was kind of an odd shade of brown. I'd check the filter and machine. Everything seemed to be working fine. Their laughter was broken up by the news director.

"Harris, do you have a minute?" Jeff Wald asked in a strong, steady voice.

"Me? Uh, yes. Hey, guys, I'll be right back," I said excitedly.

As we walked toward Jeff's office, he said, "You know, they all think you're in trouble."

"Am I?" I asked nervously. How could I be? I'd never even talked to the news director before. Oh, no, what had I done?

"Have a seat. I hear you're doing a good job for us," Jeff said.

His office was one of the only places in the newsroom that had a door. Other than that, it was pretty nondescript — not the fancy office one might expect for a man in his position. It was more of a working space than anything. And this man was definitely serious about work.

"A little bird has told me you're interested in attending the NABJ Convention later this week. You think you want to work in news?" Jeff said.

"Well, yes. The internship is great. I mean, I can see what everyone does — all the different jobs, the writers, producers, reporters and anchors. Their jobs are all so diverse," I rambled. I was gasping for breaths and babbling, I thought. This guy must have thought my oxygen supply was cut off.

"What do you want to do?" Jeff asked.

"I think I'd like to produce. And then report. I've been learning stuff over at the public access station on weekends. I can edit my own stories, and I'm pretty good at interviewing," I said confidently.

"I wish we could use you here. But the way it works is you have to cut your teeth in a smaller market. You know, make your mistakes in a town that will forgive you. Hone your skills. The NABJ is a good place to start. A lot of smaller city stations look for talent at the job fair," Jeff said. He shifted in his seat and leaned back, getting comfortable.

"We usually send a couple of people from our newsroom," he continued. He seemed to be leading up to something.

"This year, of course, it's in our city, so the attendees don't have to travel. That cuts the cost. Anyway, here's the point. How about if you go for us this year? You'll want to attend some workshops. And then there's the fair," Jeff said proudly. He undoubtedly could tell he'd just made me extremely happy. After all, I stood up suddenly.

"Yes," I said loudly. Looking around awkwardly, I sat back down.

Jeff smiled, holding back his laughter, "Well, good. We'll get you set up with a convention pass. See Bill about that."

I thanked him profusely. I practically hugged the guy. He had wished me luck, but as I walked out of his office, I knew in my heart luck had nothing to do with it. God had made a way for me to afford going to the convention. A free pass for four days!

* * * * *

So in the summer of 1990, I attended the NABJ Convention and landed a job in the small town of Greenville, North Carolina. I began working at the CBS affiliate, WNCT-TV Channel 9 in late fall of that year. In less than 18 months, a station in Kansas City invited me for an interview. And I've been at WDAF-TV4, now Fox 4, since March of 1992. I now co-anchor the weekday evening news at 6 and 10.

When I left Los Angeles for North Carolina, my friends were

skeptical. It hurt me that they couldn't be more supportive. But Liz was great. She said in that regal English accent, "Oh, they're just jealous. You're following a star in the sky — your star. It means your head has to be a little in the clouds and your feet a few inches off the ground as you jump to touch your star. Go for it. Everything will still be there when you come back to earth. You'll just be better."

She was right. My feet are on the ground most of the time. But every now and then I jump up to reach for a star. And I am definitely happier — better — having gone for it. And something else: Whenever I begin to slip into a rut, praying for courage and God's grace helps me get to the next glory in my life.

CHAPTER SIX

Sow 10 Seeds for Success

"Success is not about who you will be. It's about who you are along the way."

— H.F.

"MISS FAULKNER, how much money do you make?" asked Jerome. He was a student sitting in the front row of a crowded urban Kansas City classroom.

This was my third class visit in as many days. And, as usual, the questions among the grade-schoolers were the same. After saying they wanted to be famous, many of the children would talk about the big money they would make someday.

"If you're not makin' bank, I don't want a job like yours. But you must be rich, you're on TV," another student added.

I was candid with them.

"I've been making six figures since I was 28 years old. With God's help, hard work and determination, you can also achieve a lot. Getting there — is possible. Staying there is the tough part," I said.

"What? Who cares? Once I make the money I'll always have it. So I don't have to be rolling in the green for long," another student said.

"Besides, we've heard all the philosophy on life before. We want to know how you did it and what we can do. The teachers, they treat us like we're not going anywhere," Jerome said.

"Where are you going?" I asked.

"I'm gooooing to be rich!" shouted a student from the back of the class.

"I'm going to college, Ms. Faulkner," said Carrie, a student seated next to Jerome.

"Sounds like you have a plan. Have you prayed about it?" I asked.

"Well, I say my prayers. But what does that have to do with going to college and getting a good job? You just said anybody could do that," Carrie responded.

"Without God's grace and guidance, you may get there on your own. But why leave it to chance? Why not pray about your dreams and ask for God's intervention. Then, that success will have a firm foundation. It won't be built on shaky favors from others or lucky breaks that are unpredictable and can come with a price," I said.

"What are you talkin' about? If it happens and we make money, it's ours. No one can take it," Jerome said.

"Okay, say it happens like this. You land a job doing marketing for the Chicago Bulls —" I said.

"Forget that jazz. I wanna be on the team!" a voice from the middle of the class shouted.

"Okay, you get your dream job, and your buddy helped you get it. Then your buddy expects you to do him favors, like give him free season tickets in the fifth row! You can't even afford to do that for your own family. But you kind of owe your buddy. You have choices. You can disrespect him and tell him to get his own tickets. Or you can ante up and repay the debt," I said.

The students looked serious. They agreed that leaving life to chance was not the best way. They also agreed they'd ditch the buddy! I was a little worried that they were missing the point. But then they asked for a list of tips to write down in their notebooks — ways to live a plan that God was involved in. Carrie, the college-minded student, said she'd rather owe God a debt of gratitude than some "two-bit, greedy homegirl." I guess they got the point.

I shared with them the idea that life is a garden that you sow. It can either be beautiful or in great despair. And there are ten seeds we can sow for success — the kind of success that God has planned for us. They liked the first seed.

SEED #1: HAVE FUN

Having spent some time in the company of a friend's two-year-old son, I've learned a valuable lesson: *Having fun* is essential to achieving our goals.

My friends Cassie and Bill were potty training Bryant. It wasn't easy. Bryant had become so stressed out about not messing up his pants that it was all he could think about. He was moody. He wouldn't play with anyone. He had just about stopped talking altogether.

The saddest part was that every day, at some point, it would happen. He'd lose control and wet his pants.

Cassie and Bill tried everything to keep him from being so frustrated. They didn't scold him for making a mistake because they knew how hard he was trying. Cassie told me she was riddled with guilt. She even considered putting a diaper back on him and letting him go back to being a baby. She said, at least then, Bryant would be happy. By the way, Cassie was about eight months pregnant, and she pretty much worried about everything.

One day, a new family moved into the house next door to Cassie and Bill. The new family's four-year-old daughter quickly became the talk of the subdivision. Apparently she had appeared on some soap opera and in a few TV commercials. The neighbor parents made a big deal out of it. And all the neighbor kids wanted to play with Christina, the actress.

"I don't think Bryant likes girls," Cassie said into the receiver. She had the telephone cradled between her right ear and shoulder. She was chopping vegetables for dinner.

"Are you crying over this?" I asked.

"No, of course not. I'm sniffling because I'm chopping an onion. But I am worried. I mean, I don't care if he's gay, I just don't want him to be anti-social," Cassie said between sniffles.

"We are talking about Bryant, right?"

"Yes, my wonderful little boy — a homosexual. And maybe a social misfit," Cassie snorted loudly.

"Those are some big labels to be putting on a two-year-old. What's goin' on?"

"Well, the new little star, ya know, KRISTEENAH." Obviously, Cassie didn't care for the new neighbor girl, or at least she didn't like her new-found popularity. "Her mother brought her over to meet Bryant and to invite us to a housewarming party this weekend. Bryant took one look at the little girl and ran screaming through the house," Cassie said.

"Well, is she ugly?"

"Come on, Harris, this is serious."

Still laughing, I said, "All right, go on."

"It's just that with a new baby coming, I want Bryant to be well-adjusted."

"You spend every waking moment with the kid. Take him to a daycare and let him learn to get along. And you go do something for yourself. Take one of those cooking classes you used to love so much."

"Oh, Harris. You're so '90s."

"Imagine that. It is 1997."

"You're getting frustrated with me, aren't you? Well, Bill wants to send him to a shrink," Cassie said in a sad voice.

"Now, Cass, don't start crying. It's not the end of the world if Bryant doesn't get potty trained right now."

"What are you talking about? I'm telling you he's becoming a social misfit, and you're talking about pee."

"Cass! Stop calling him names. And this *is* about potty training. The little guy's so stressed out he can hardly breathe."

"So you're saying I'm an unfit mother," Cassie said defensively.

If you hadn't noticed before now, it's probably becoming very clear. Cassie is the last of the great over-reactors — next to her husband Bill, that is. He loses it on a regular basis. But you won't find any two people who are more loving, generous or likeable. It was time for me to take action. BE HONEST.

"Cass, get a life. If it weren't for Bill's social commitments through his work and my coaxing you out of the house, you'd be borderline anti-social yourself. So don't dwell on Bryant. I know you're pregnant. And you don't have a lot of energy right now. But get out and do something for yourself and take Bryant to daycare. Even if it's just a couple of times a week."

"Why am I asking you? You don't even have kids. But what you're saying does make sense."

"It's just instinct."

"I'll try it your way."

"Good. Call me and let me know how the first visit goes."

"All right, but I hope it's not a disaster." Cassie's famous last words.

* * * * *

"Harris! If you're there, pick up! It's Cass. It's an —"

"Cass, is that you? I'm just walking in the door. Hold on. Let me turn off the alarm. Okay." I put down the bags I was carrying and collapsed into a chair in the kitchen.

"Harris, I'm calling you from a tow-truck. They're hauling the Volvo away. Bryant's still at that daycare center, and it closes in a half-hour."

"I'm on my way." I slammed down the phone and then frantically picked it up again.

"Oh, no! Cass?"

"I'm still here. It's on Quivira and 79th Street. Thanks. And, by the way, meet me at St. Joseph's Hospital. It's time."

"Oh, now! Try to stay calm. I'll call Bill and we'll meet you there!"

* * * * *

"Hello, I'm Harris Faulkner. Here to pick up Bryant Simms," I said out of breath.

"Yes. His mother called a bit ago. Is she okay?" asked the daycare instructor.

"Oh, yeah. She was just in labor. There's Bryant," I said, walking away from the instructor who looked stunned by what I said. She went to gather Bryant's things. And I had been spotted.

"Hawwas!" Bryant looked happier than I'd seen him in weeks. He ran over, and we hugged.

"Hey, big guy. How's it going?" We walked over to a couple of his new buddies.

"Wow, what's all this?" I asked.

"We're building a shopping mall," said one of the older children. He carefully added a block to a tall stack that formed an "H."

"Miss Faulkner, he didn't use any of these, but here's Bryant's bag of diapers. If he's potty trained, why does his mom send diapers? Well, it's none of my business," the instructor said.

Potty trained, I thought.

"Bryant, I'm taking you to see your mommy." I picked him up and grabbed his bag. He waved good-bye to his friends. Then, still in my arms, he looked up at me and said so proudly, "I make potty now."

"I'll take Bryant. This little guy has to go too," said a young instructor who had a little boy about Bryant's age, standing at her side. Off they went to the restroom.

* * * * *

Bryant talked all the way to the hospital, or at least he thought he was talking. I made out a few words here and there. What was perfectly clear, though, was how much fun he had had. I hesitated to bring up the subject, but curiosity was killing me.

"So how did it go with making potty today?" I asked in his language.

"Fun! Hambugger! Hambugger!"

Yes, we had passed McDonald's. I gathered from Bryant's answer to my question that he was so distracted by all the great stuff to do at daycare that he didn't have time to worry about meeting his goal of keeping his pants dry. And perhaps somehow one of the instructors or the other kids had made going to the potty an enjoyable experience.

* * * * *

These days, Cassie takes both of her boys to daycare three days a week, while she works out at the gym and researches her dream to start a catering business. Both of the boys are happily potty trained, on most days anyway.

* * * * *

Get this: *Having fun* helps us relieve stress and open our minds to tackling our goals and issues with freshness and energy. And gaining a little distance from a problem, challenge or dream can give us a greater perspective on the less appealing tasks. For example, if you must work 12 hours a day to accomplish your goal, schedule some time to laugh and have fun. It's important to let go. You just may be better mentally prepared for the next 12-hour shift. Life is about balance, and as little Bryant showed me, the opposite of "must do" is "must play."

SEED #2: SURROUND YOURSELF WITH POSITIVE PEOPLE

From the National Football League to a local bar-b-que cook-off, many people achieve their greatest accomplishments as members of teams. Here's an odd, but effective example of a team. When my girlfriends go out to a nightclub, they share the goal of spotting cute guys. Their method depends on teamwork. For instance, when Kellie meets a guy with potential, Max and Suzanne go to work, doing nothing short of an FBI investigation. If the guy answers a couple of their questions in a way that displeases Kellie, she simply coughs three times. Upon that cue, her team members begin "Operation Ditch the Dude." That can be anything from suddenly going to the ladies room together, to one of them shrieking, "Eek! There's a mouse on the dance floor!" causing momentary pandemonium. Of course, playing my usual role as devil's advocate, I question their method because the last time either of them dated a guy longer than six weeks, Reagan was president.

Teams are everywhere. Astronauts on board the space shuttle, actors dressed as characters at Disney World, flight attendants — all teams working toward common goals. Although Michael Jordan is the star, without his teammates there would have been no "Da Bulls." Not to mention, without a team — Jordan wouldn't have those championship rings.

So it follows, forming a team can greatly boost your potential for success. But it has to be the right team. And in this case, the shared goal is not scoring points. Rather it is to foster a positive environment where it's safe to talk about your dreams with others who are also looking for success.

In Chapter 4, I talk about getting started in television news and the positive influence of my friend, Liz Warren. You might call Liz a key part of TEAM HARRIS. That's right, I pictured my success as being the result of a collaborative effort — one that would need some integral players. That's not to say I chose my friends merely on the basis of what they could do for me. Rather, I pursued friendships with people who had similar values and attitudes and with a quality that I lacked. For example, Liz was a positive thinker, ambitious and meticulous. We had those things in common. But Liz was more reality-based than me. I helped her dream, and she helped me stay in the real world. We were good team members because we complemented each other.

We should all have at least one "Liz" in our lives. Of course, you also must *be* a good team member. For instance, my closest buddies will tell you I'm a good person to have around in a crisis. I'm able to stay calm and focused when others are in trouble. I've learned that in order to attract and keep friends that form a positive team, we must also have something to offer.

There are all sorts of ways to meet people who have a healthy outlook on life. I've been most successful meeting them at church, volunteering with charitable organizations and community groups and at the mall. Some of the most positive people around are those trying to sell regular-priced retail merchandise when it's not the Christmas shopping season. And they still manage to smile. You may not always buy from them, but you have to admire their tenacity.

Please don't misunderstand, the goal here is not to befriend pushy people, but those who believe that something can be done even when the odds are against it. Once you've formed a positive team, make time for it. It's important to plan activities that will allow you to discuss and explore each other's dreams and all the possibilities there are to achieving those dreams. Let those closest to you know how they can help you. For example, when I began writing this book, my friend Ed Crony and I were on a hiking trip in Breckenridge, Colorado. Ed took great pleasure in pouring over the early pages, looking for grammatical and spelling errors. But his main purpose was to tell me honestly if I was wasting my time. Ed was poised to give constructive criticism. But his first words were, "This doesn't suck!" That was an excellent sign.

Aside from knowing me better than just about anyone, including my family, Ed is a senior promotions producer for a TV station in Denver. If anyone is qualified to give advice on a manuscript, it's a guy who spends all day writing and coming up with ways to get people to watch his product. Ed is a pivotal member of TEAM HARRIS.

* * * * *

Get this: Mine is a small team — just a handful of people whom I trust, respect and find motivating on many levels. That's the idea for your immediate circle. Next, move on to forming a separate ring of positive role models and professionals who can help you achieve your goal or dream. My outer ring, or TEAM HARRIS II, consists of the pastor at my church, my broadcast agent, news anchors at the network level and others. These are people who can give you advice or help point you in the direction of an opportunity. Remember, someone did it for them, and one day you'll be in the position to help a dreamer along the way. Now, you have a small circle of close friends with whom you share positive, stimulating conversations and experiences. Then there's your outer ring of professionals or experts to help keep you informed and focused. You're ready for the next SEED.

SEED #3: DO YOUR DREAM
(Taken from "Finding Real Success" speech, at Hallmark, Inc., 1994)

Good morning, everyone. And welcome to this special day for employees in our humble division of Hallmark. Today we have a guest speaker you may all recognize from the evening news. She's Harris Faulkner, co-anchor of the news at 6 and 10 for Fox Four.

Harris is going to talk with us today about finding real success in our lives. Just a little bit about our speaker now. Harris began her career working as a reporter and morning anchor in Greenville, North Carolina. One year later, she joined WDAF-TV in March of 1992 as a consumer reporter. Soon thereafter, she began co-anchoring the news on a fill-in basis. In 1993, she was named co-anchor with Phil Witt. While her schedule is full as a journalist, Harris also volunteers in Kansas City communities as a motivational speaker, at schools, churches and corporations, like ours.

Harris will talk today about enriching your life by giving you examples from her own. Please help me give a warm welcome to Harris Faulkner.

(audience applause)

Thank you so much. You know, as she was reading my biography, I realized some of that stuff I've never heard before! As she said, you may recognize me from the evening news ... unless, of course, you watch Channel 9!

Okay, let's get started. I'm seldom at a loss for words, but I do pause every now and then. So if you think of something, if you have a question or if something just hits you that works, raise your hand. In fact, by a show of hands, who wants to find "real" success? That's almost everyone, except for this one woman down front — who seems to be overjoyed about the snacks at her table!

Real success is not about your salary or your status in the neighborhood. It's not about the car you drive or the clothes your kids wear. Real success is not some place you arrive at after some undetermined amount of hard work or dedication. It is not a destination.

Real success is a journey — something that takes a lifetime to achieve.

I saw a bumper sticker on the car in front of me the other day, and it made such an impression on me I wrote it down. I do that, just take notes at a moment's notice. It's a habit that validates that little news notebook and pen I carry around constantly.

Anyway, the sticker said, "Do your dream." Now, I thought about that. And a little pessimism came out — what if you can't make your dream come true? What if life hasn't given you an opportunity? What if ... YOU'RE NOT DOING YOUR DREAM?

Then it hit me — don't worry, I didn't hit the car in front of me. But a big rush came over me because I realized how basic and true that statement is.

"Do your dream." In your home, when you're alone, when you're with family or friends ... just do it. Don't wait for anything. Sooner or later, "doing your dream" will pay off.

And be careful of your attitude toward and how you talk about your dream. You must know your dream is tied to a higher power, a divine order. For some of you this may be God, for others, just think of it as a positive power that you can tap into by keeping pure, positive thoughts about your dream. Success is made from the inside out. So what we believe has a direct effect on how we think about ourselves and others. Our beliefs affect our actions and our dreams. People are different in how and what they worship, but as long as their belief influences them to treat others well and inspires them to do their best, then that belief is crucial.

So it follows, your mind is powerful. If you focus on a positive source, your ability to take positive action may be a lot easier. And to find real success, drawing on positive energy with your mind is necessary.

Once you have your mind in tune with a positive source, the next step is to identify your dream. If you're not sure, make a list of things you're both good at and that you enjoy doing. I call these your gifts. We all have gifts. One of mine is home decorating. My friends always say when there's a question about taste or ideas in decor, ask Harris. Another of mine is fashion. I was a model for most of my grade school years and voted best-dressed in high school. While living in the San Francisco Bay area, my parents drove me into the city for modeling jobs — some runway work, but mostly print advertisements for local publications. In college, I was a swimsuit model in the Women of Santa Barbara calendar. That helped me pay some bills. These days, my gift in fashion has to do with dressing for the nightly news and for formal charity engagements. I'm not a fashion designer for a living, but designing some of the clothes I wear allows me to exercise one of my gifts.

The point here is that you may not make money or form a career out of each of your gifts, but it helps to identify them so you can narrow them down to the dream you'd like to see come true.

For example, say you have a gift in the kitchen. You can cook anything. That may lead to a dream of having your own catering business. Do your dream! Cook for everybody you know. Perfect recipes. Cater friends' parties for just the cost of the food. Get good at your dream, so when an opportunity comes along, and it will, you will have been doing your dream for so long, the only difference will be getting paid.

If your dream is to become an actor — ACT. Join church plays, a local theater group or whatever. Be willing to ACT for free. When an opportunity comes along — and it will — you will have been doing your dream … preparing for your big break.

Get your mouth in line with your mind and body. When people ask you what you do for a living — don't tell them about your job. Tell them about your dream and talk about it in the present. Say, "I have a career in catering, but I also work at Hallmark Cards as an assistant." Or say, "I have a career in management at Hallmark Cards, but I also work in the mailroom." Attitude is everything. If you believe you can, you will. By the way, since you may be wondering, my newest dream is to write books. Watch those bookshelves!

You heard me say that you must be willing to work for free. In the television news business, we call this an internship. It's the basic idea of an apprenticeship — observing or taking on limited responsibilities for the purpose of learning a skill or about a certain job. This is an old workforce tradition, and you're never too old to try it. Just about any workplace could use some short-term help that it doesn't have to pay for. So answer the phones or run errands in a dream workplace and absorb what you can. This is especially helpful if you're thinking of starting your own business. See how others are doing it, and pay for that education with your labor. You may realize that it's not for you and would have lost nothing in the long run.

While doing your dream, you may run across someone who can help you. Don't be intimidated to ask for help, but temper that with good judgment. You don't want to seem desperate. If someone is in a position to open a door or give you information, just ask. If they say "no," move on.

Doing your dream is the only way to find real success. If you don't follow your heart, you'll always wonder if you could have, should have. And you may miss an incredible opportunity to be happy. But you may also miss out on a way to help others. By following my dream to be a journalist, I've uncovered stories about people in trouble, impacting their lives with my work. It doesn't always happen like that. But when it does, I realize how much I can make a difference by doing my dream.

A final thought: Our dreams may change throughout the course of our lives. That's why doing them is important. They keep us going forward — positively in motion and positively focused. I once dreamed of being an accountant. Through that line of work, I met a news anchor in Los Angeles who was writing a book. She took me to work with her one day — and there was born a new dream. Who knows where my dream job at Channel 4 will lead in the future, but I'll keep doing it as long as it's in my heart to do so.

Thank you very much for inviting me to speak with you this morning. I'll answer questions from the audience now, but first — I challenge you to do your dream — start right now. Tell the person next to you what it is.

* * * * *

The above speech was one of the first I ever gave in Kansas City. I was nervous, but excited to share my lessons about success. Many people in the audience came up to me after the speech to say they'd taken notes on my ideas and were going to do their dreams immediately.

* * * * *

Get this: There's no magic word or action anyone can take to achieve success. But there is a place that everyone should start. That place is right now, right where you stand. Keep your body and your mind clear of negativity and don't quit!

SEED #4: WORK HARD AND STUDY HARDER

My dad loves to watch ESPN *Sportscenter.* I must confess to watching it, too. Sometimes I watch the same taped broadcast more than once. A couple of years ago, when the Chicago Bulls were in the final playoffs of the NBA, I actually stuck a VHS tape in to record a portion of *Sportscenter*. What was so captivating? The Bulls had lost a key game early in the series, and the star player Michael Jordan was interviewed and asked if the team was in trouble. Jordan said, "It was one loss. I've lost before. The thing is now, we just can't let one loss become two. We'll have to work harder and remember that we've been here before and what we've learned."

I met Jordan once, years before that *Sportscenter* interview. His annual golf tournament was held in Greenville, North Carolina, the first television market where I worked on air. After a news conference, in a brief conversation he told me he liked playing golf because it tested his knowledge as much as his physical ability. He said a lot of people can do the work, but you have to know the game if you want to win often.

Other professional athletes have told me the same thing. My friend Kellen Winslow says you have to know the game you play or don't bother stepping onto the field. Winslow definitely knew the game of football. In 1995, he was inducted into the NFL Hall of Fame after incredible catches he made as a tight end for the San Diego Chargers back in the 1980s. Kellen has talked about the greatest players studying more than the playbook. He says the true champions study the game's history — knowing the triumphs and sacrifices of past heroes.

Jordan and Winslow share a philosophy which applies to anyone trying to succeed. Let's apply it to a dream to make fashion accessories. First, you might want to learn how other designers made it big. Learn what's sold well in the past and how it compares with your product. Check out your local and global competition — the Internet is a good tool for this. Then look to the future. For example, talk with young teenagers about what they like and don't like in the fashions they see adults wearing. No doubt, it will take hard work to break into the fashion industry, but you'll be working up a sweat for nothing if you don't study the industry first.

Even after being in TV news for more than eight years, I continue to study my craft. In 1996, I competed with other journalists to get into the Poynter Institute for Media Studies. In a course on advanced reporting, I learned to take my storytelling and live on-the-scene reporting skills to the next level. I took time off from my anchor job to do this. Some people said they thought it was odd than an evening news anchor would want to go back to school to learn about being a better reporter. To me, anchors should be the best reporters on the news team — capable of covering any store live in the field, away from the scripts and cushion of the anchor desk. My game is journalism. It takes hard work to stay sharp at all the skills required for that game. And even when I work long, unpredictable hours in the field covering news of a building explosion or a plane crash, it's my knowledge of my game that sets my stories apart from others.

Most people agree hard work is necessary, but few people want to do the most difficult job of all — study. This is different from school. You don't get a grade ... you get to be considered good. And if you study hard, you may be considered one of the best at what you choose to do.

* * * * *

Get this: There are a multitude of tools out there for researching your dream. Your local library is a great place to start. You'll find historical materials, reference guides, and in some larger cities libraries offer Internet access. Check periodicals for workshops and seminars in your area. Attend those events and take copious notes.

SEED #5: BE TAMPER-RESISTANT

Around and around the top spins. You can't just turn the top to open a tamper-resistant bottle of aspirin. You have to apply just the right amount of pressure at the right moment — turning and pressing down simultaneously. For a child this is a difficult maneuver. It's too much work. Soon a curious little one will cast aside the stubborn bottle of aspirin for something a little easier to manipulate. That's why they make the bottle that way, to keep the child away from what's inside. This is how I illustrate this seed for success.

Our good attitude is like the aspirin inside the bottle. And the child trying to open the bottle is like the devil or the evil side of people that want to mess with our good attitude. No, this does not reflect how I feel about children! It's just a way to make a point.

How can we tell when the devil has popped the top on us? We start to complain. Suddenly, our positive outlook grows negative. We find fault in others and ourselves. We feel insecure. And generally our mouths begin to get us in trouble.

For example, say you're not happy on your job, but you're trying to have a good attitude because you know in your heart that's what God wants. The devil can't stand this. You're minding your own business, trying to see the good in your circumstances. Maybe you got passed over for a promotion. Or maybe you're looking for a better job, but you have to keep the one you have to pay the bills. Whatever the case, you're trying to have a good attitude. The devil, bothered by your righteousness, rears his ugly head. He may use someone near you. For instance, it may be a co-worker who coerces you into gossiping about people in the office. Or worse, that co-worker may get you to talk about all the things on the job that are bugging you. One conversation won't hurt. But say you begin commiserating every day with that co-worker on just how bad everything is. Soon you're spending more time complaining than you are working. THIS IS TROUBLE.

Others around you, maybe even your boss, may label you and treat you accordingly. So it follows, your *bad* attitude may be the very reason why you don't get a promotion or a raise or a better job.

You have to be tougher than that. You must be *tamper-resistant*. Make it difficult for the devil to shake up your good attitude. When someone approaches you with gossip, tell that person you're busy. Say "no" to an invitation to go to lunch with that co-worker who likes to moan and groan about everything. If you're not happy on the job, ask God for his grace and guidance to work out something better for you. And in the meantime, carry on doing what you can to stay on a righteous path. If you get nothing else out of this book, remember: Complaining, gossiping and being negative will change nothing. Except maybe you and your relationship with God. God does not favor complainers. If you doubt it, watch the people around you. The movers and the shakers seldom are the ones cavorting around the office coffee pot. The truly successful people are too busy trying to accomplish their goals. And the complainers usually are not running the company. That's because they don't have the time or the energy. Being negative is time-consuming and physically draining.

* * * * *

Get this: Here's an exercise for you. For five minutes, think about all the things you can do to prepare for or to make your dream come true. In other words, think positively. While you are just thinking, someone else is living that way, and succeeding.

SEED #6: VOLUNTEER / SHARE YOUR BLESSINGS

You get what you put out. What goes around, comes around. These are a couple of statements many people believe are true. If they are, then life must hand back the energy that we put out. That's why volunteering or sharing God's gifts is important. It's a way of putting out positive energy — energy that will make its way back to you.

While you're struggling and toiling to realize your dream, you may experience what I call "empty time." That's when it appears nothing is happening. You're just kind of in a holding pattern. Don't lose your faith. God works in His own time, not ours. He may be working things out for you, and that's the time when you must stay fruitful in your labors. Notice, I didn't say to stay busy — I said stay fruitful. This empty time is in a small way a test of our faith. So don't just sit by, be bold in your faith — push on and get your mind off yourself. Do something for someone else and expect nothing in return. Put in some hours at a soup kitchen. Explore outreach or charity programs at your job. Perhaps you can get more involved in a cause that you usually only give money to. Volunteer your services at your local animal shelter. Shelters often need someone to clean up dogs and cats for adoption. Volunteer at a retirement facility, reading aloud to residents or just being a good listener.

Again, the key is to focus on helping others whose dream may just be to have a stranger show them some compassion.

The experience you have volunteering may help prepare you for your dream. At the very least, you may learn something new or encounter an interesting person. And again you're being fruitful in your actions.

Volunteering takes on a different level of importance after you begin succeeding. At that point, it becomes a responsibility to foster others on their way to finding success.

Share the news of your blessings by speaking at local grade schools during their career days. Host a high school class tour at your job. Working at a TV station, I'm often called upon by teachers to host a tour of our studios for small groups of high school seniors. It's a way to give them a chance to see just how TV news works. Quite a few teenagers have told me, "Ms. Faulkner, your job isn't as glamorous as it looks on TV. Is the newsroom always this stressful?"

Also, sowing the seed of volunteering is kind of like getting a little extra credit in the spiritual realm — it's sort of a cosmic brownie point. And that certainly can't hurt anything.

* * * * *

Get this: A word of caution: There's a catch with this seed. Don't go around bragging about the good you're doing. That only takes away from your credibility as a volunteer. Some people will only do a favor or help someone in need if they think they'll be recognized or praised for it. It's okay to do positive things for the purpose of contributing to the flow of good energy. But I believe we can do the right things for the wrong reasons, and that basically cancels out that spiritual extra credit.

SEED #7: STAY PHYSICALLY FIT

Getting into shape takes your mind and your body. Most people know that. You can't do one leg lift or run one mile unless you put your mind to it. But there's another ingredient to achieving fitness that many people don't consider. Your soul or your will, which I use interchangeably, determines just how fit you'll be.

If being in great shape meant you had to run 20 laps through a difficult obstacle course, would you finish? With your mind and body, racing around 10 times might sound doable. But the slighter your will, the tougher the remaining laps would be. That 11th lap would be painful. The 13th lap would seem endless. Number 14 would be nearly impossible to complete. For some of you, lap 15 would be about all she wrote. After all, 15 out of 20 would mean you were at least in good shape. Your mind would concede that your body had had enough. Completing the final five laps would have to come from someplace else — your soul.

The soul of a winner is packed with "want to" and is very unfamiliar with quitting. A few of us would cross the finish line after 20 laps, with nothing more intact than our will to do so. The course would crush our bodies, entangle minds, but build our will. That's where you want to be, building your will. Your physical strength and endurance are a place to practice building this part of your character. This doesn't mean you should spend hours at the gym or torture yourself by running marathons, unless you like that. No, this is a lesson about testing your will before life has a chance to.

I think better, have fewer aches and pains, and all around I'm a happier person when I'm working out regularly. And each time I complete a work-out, no matter how tough or for how long, I've strengthened my will to do the right thing for myself over watching TV, eating ice cram, gossiping with my girlfriends or just plain wasting time.

Unless you're perfect, physically challenging yourself builds character that can help you find true success in other areas in your life. Besides that, most of us feel better when we look better!

* * * * *

Get this: The price is mind, body and soul. The reward is

staying physically fit, which builds character and helps you exude confidence. Whenever I see a person who is horribly out of
shape, yet capable of doing something about it, I wonder what
other areas of their life are out of control. Can they handle the
stresses and nuances that go along with finding success and making their dreams come true? How do they deal with responsibility if they cannot make the choice to put down sugar-coated snack
number 10 for the day? Maybe potential employers think this way,
too. Just a thought.

Not everyone's body-type will allow for a thin, muscular phy-
sique. However, working to the best of your ability with what
you have is the goal.

SEED #8: PRAY FOR COURAGE AND GOD'S GRACE

Have you checked out WWW.BIBLE.COM. It's one of my favorite websites. It has a search engine that can help you find
pertinent scriptures for your life. And it can search by topic. One
day I looked up the word "grace." It was listed so many times in
the Bible the search exceeded the time my server would allow
… kicking me off the site. In other words, God's grace is tried
and tested true by some of His earliest disciples and teachers.
Simply put, God can do things in our lives we cannot. And praying for His grace can better prepare us for life's toughest moments and greatest accomplishments.

In the chapter "Getting Unstuck," you read about how I was
trying to make the unlikely transition from accounting to TV news.
Even though I was living out God's plan for my life, there were
hurdles along the way. For me, finding a way to work in television in a setting that would allow me to learn from some of the
best journalists in the nation took some backbone. I had to be
courageous enough to convince news management to hire a post-
graduate for what was basically a paid college internship. Then I
needed the energy to work my day job and work another six
hours a night at the TV station and work weekends at a public
access station learning the technical side of the business, such as
editing videotape. I had faith in seeing my dream through, but it

was only possible with God's grace.

Your obstacles may be very different. One example: You're raising a family, working and trying to pursue your dream, all at the same time. The second example: You live in a town or city which does not offer you an opportunity in your chosen pursuit.

In the first case, it will take courage to tell your family and/or employer you need to make time for yourself. Maybe you discover the only extra time is late at night or before dawn. Pray for God's grace to have the energy to do this.

In the second case, you may need to be courageous enough to leave your home and go where the opportunities are. That could involve leaving friends, loved ones, a good-paying job. You may even end up creating a long-distance relationship if you're attached. Doing this won't be easy. Praying for courage and God's grace will help you do the things you need to, even when they seem impossible.

That brings me to the next point. What does impossible mean to you? If it means giving up when 10 or 12 things come against you in your success journey, you may as well quit now. You must be courageous enough to persevere when your goal seems far from reach.

Let's play the "What if" game. My friend Nick Lowery, now retired from the National Football League, once told me he tried out for more than two dozen teams. At the time, there were only 28 NFL teams. He got turned down from nearly every one. Today, Nick will likely go into the NFL Hall of Fame for his years of record-setting success with the Kansas City Chiefs.

What if Nick had given up after the first 10 teams told him no? When the struggle toward your dream gets to be too great, pray for courage to face rejection and God's grace to press on.

* * * * *

Get this: There is no glass-smooth, perfectly straight road for most of us. But the bumps and roadblocks along the way shape us according to God's plan, and they make us stronger. As our dreams become reality, they have more meaning as we've gained perspective on the true cost of sticking with something.

SEED #9: TRAVEL

Many people believe travel is a luxury, reserved for the rich and famous. But a change in our environment is good for all of us. And it can be very affordable. Just start by taking little trips.

Travel begins just outside your front door. If you haven't met your neighbors across the street, go there. Then leave your neighborhood and visit the rest of the city in which you live. Go to any older areas to learn about the history of your home city. Visit the newer areas to glimpse the future. From there, plan a series of short trips to other cities in your state.

Travel involves seeing new things and, more importantly, meeting people who are different from you. The idea is to get out of your comfort zone and try to see the world from a more experienced and enlightened perspective. I think young children do this instinctively. Maybe that's why they're always trying to crawl, walk or run in every direction.

When it comes to working on your professional goals, you may find some key people along the way. I've discovered dreamers often congregate in some of the same places. At my favorite travel destinations, I almost always bump into another person staring into the ocean waves, contemplating how they will achieve their goals. Travel can lead you to some motivating people — maybe even someone who shares your dream.

Lest you feel your budget will limit your travel to the states you can reach by car, that's not a detriment. The United States is the most diverse nation in the world with plenty of low-cost accommodations and activities from corner to corner. With 3,681,760 miles to cover, you're sure to see plenty of beautiful views and meet a lot of people. And you'll undoubtedly collect interesting stories to tell when you return home. In fact, travel can make you appreciate home a little more.

* * * * *

Get this: You need to be two things when you travel — flexible and open-minded. Plans on the road are seldom glitch-free, so you must be flexible and go with the flow. And meeting people whose culture, language or social views are different from your own is nearly inevitable. If you open your mind and your heart and they do the same, the exchange will be unforgettable. After all, the value of traveling is as much about the experiences and information you give as it is about that which you gain.

SEED #10: HAVE A THANKFUL HEART

Imagine traveling through a beautiful forest with me as your companion. You and I are on a mission in search of the Legendary Purple Door, behind which all dreams are kept. When we find the door, we must get it to open so that we can see how all of our unanswered prayers and unrealized fantasies will come true.

After hours of wandering about the forest thick with trees and brilliantly colored flowers, we find the Legendary Purple Door. And there's a strange character standing outside the door waiting to greet passersby with special instructions. He's a whimsical look-ing fellow, short, only about four feet tall, but he appears to be about 40 years old. He's wearing a red velvet jacket with black knickers, plaid socks and black shiny shoes. His hair is golden blonde and his eyes are a piercing azure.

In his little hands, he holds a large book. The book is bound in leather. The edges of its pages are painted gold so they shim-mer as they're turned.

"My name is Dugan," the man says. He speaks with an ac-cent, sort of an Irish-Spanish mix. "I hold the answers to the ques-tions you'll ask. But only you hold the key to getting in."

Who is this guy, the Riddler? It figures, you and I would en-counter history's only wizard with a smart aleck attitude. But we take the bait.

"What great task must we perform to crack the lock on the door?" you ask. Good question. Glad I'm with you.

"No task, nothing like that," Dugan shoots back.

You persist, "Surely there's a battle to be fought and won. Perhaps there are hot coals to walk across. Or maybe even some demon we must destroy?"

Demon! Hey, partner, settle down. How 'bout we leave the monsters out of it!

"No task, no demons, nothing like that," Dugan says, speaking a bit slower this time.

This guy seems a couple of sandwiches short of a picnic. Maybe I'd better take a turn at asking the questions.

"Okay, Duncan," I say.

"It's Dugan!" he says abruptly.

"Sorry, dude. Look, Dugan buddy, what's it gonna take to open the door? I've got a newscast to anchor, let's get to it."

"You do news in the forest?" Dugan quips.

"Well, no. I just thought —"

"Status won't help you here. If you want to see your dreams come true, you must be willing to do three things with feeling," Dugan says.

Now we're getting somewhere.

Dugan begins turning the pages in the big leather-bound book. He stops and begins to read aloud.

"No man or woman shall enter the Grand Grape Door without uttering the magical words with feeling."

"Okay, we'll say them. Just tell us what they are," you demand. Not so fast, partner of mine. Those words could be anything. We might have to promise to live on another planet — only inhabited by men.

On second thought, "Yeah, what are those words we have to say?" I ask.

"You must refrain from interrupting me," Dugan continues. "After you utter the magical words, you must promise to do two things as often as you can." Dugan pauses, then begins again. "Are you ready for the key to entering the door to your dreams?"

"No, Bob Barker, we've just been standing here to hang out with you." Ouch, you're getting a little testy. And for that matter, who wouldn't be anxious to learn the key to all that we desire?

"Very well. The two words you must say often with feeling are THANK and YOU. The tricky part — the two things you must do. First, you must show kindness to those around you. And you must truly be grateful for the blessings you already have before expecting anything more," Dugan says this all in one breath. He gasps for air at the end and smiles. His eyes twinkle.

Obviously there are others who have gone before you and me and failed. Dugan knows the task at hand is much simpler to say than do for most people. Suddenly, you take charge.

"I understand. Humbly before all who can hear the sound of my voice, I say THANK YOU for my blessings. And knowing what my talents are, I pledge to assist others with kindness in any way that I can. And I will take nothing for granted. Even if this door of dreams never opens, I'm grateful for all that I have now," you say.

Wow! You're awesome. Glad I brought you. Look! The door is opening. And we're going inside. Hey, there's "good health in old age." That must be one of your dreams. But wait, there's "a beautiful wedding with that cute guy on *Baywatch*." You guessed it, that's one of mine.

As we leave, the Grand Grape Door closes behind us. You and I are elated to have seen the dreams come true that lie ahead for us. On our way out of the forest, we pass a couple of guys sitting on a log. They're complaining about the weather, money and other stuff they don't have …

One looks up at us, "You two losers get turned away, too?"

Before we can answer, the other guy says, "Yeah, who can be thankful when nothing good ever happens to us? Pass me that sandwich, would ya?" His friend hands him the food.

You say, "Well, you're not going hungry. You look healthy, and at least you made it to the big door and tried to get in. Some people never find it. You have a lot to be thankful for."

The second guy retorts, "What do you know? You're not carrying any riches. You didn't get in."

You respond, "Yes, I did, and the greatest gift of all is knowing what can happen in the future, and in the meantime that all I have to do is hold gratitude and generosity in my heart."

You are so smart. And don't you love a story with a happy ending, especially when you're in it!

* * * * *

Get this: The moral of this story asks a question: Why should we be blessed with more if we don't appreciate what we have?

SOW 10 SEEDS FOR SUCCESS

I usually don't advocate ripping up books. Here's an exception. I've put the *10 Seeds* on one page. Cut out this page along the dotted line and place it where you can reference it often.

1. *Have Fun*

2. *Surround Yourself With Positive People*

3. *Do Your Dream*

4. *Work Hard and Study Harder*

5. *Be Tamper-Resistant*

6. *Volunteer / Share Your Blessings*

7. *Stay Physically Fit*

8. *Pray for Courage and God's Grace*

9. *Travel*

10. *Have a Thankful Heart*

While you sow your seeds for success, you live in America where the potential exists for anyone's dreams to come true. You follow a God who promises through Him, all things are possible. And by living out the above ten seeds, you'll be more positive and more productive ... making you unstoppable!

CHAPTER SEVEN

How to Find God's Plan for Your Life

"THOSE SHOES DON'T MATCH," my mother said. My parents were in town. My mother was putting a pan of biscuits in the oven when she looked up and noticed my outfit.

"Oh, Shirley, leave her alone," my father said, with the same expression he wears most of the time — a slight, pleasant smile. He's a tall, thin man with gray hair that shows just a little of the dark brown he hasn't seen since his twenties. My father sat in a high-backed chair at the tall, round kitchen table watching a small television set that shared a counter with the telephone, toaster and blender. He was captivated by highlights on ESPN, breaking his silence periodically to emote like a teenager, screaming at the TV set and often threatening to climb in and coach the game himself.

"Take those shoes off," my mother continued. She was now searching for her cigarettes.

"Mom, they're part of my plan," I responded, walking around the house collecting items for my purse … my keys on the dining room table, wallet on the kitchen counter, etc.

"What's your speech on today, the horrors of bad fashion?" She actually had resorted to heckling me.

"Shirley, be quiet, they're showing last night's …" My father's voice trailed off as he focused in on a play they were showing in slow-motion. He was re-living a game he had already watched and getting the scoop on the stuff he had shouted through. He looked away from the TV to see what my mom was so upset about.

"Wow, those are tacky." My dad quickly looked at my outfit and the mismatched shoes and turned back toward the TV at breakneck speed.

"Dad, not you, too," I said. He smiled, but didn't take his eyes off the highlights.

"Mom, these shoes are a perfect tool in my plan to teach this junior high school student body I'm visiting today about preparedness," I explained. She was not impressed.

"You look like you're prepared for the world to end in the dark," she quipped. How amusing. She hadn't been this annoyed with me in years, not since high school probably. It seemed a shame to waste such a special mother-daughter moment, but I had to come clean. An extra pair of shoes that matched my outfit were packed in a bag for me to change into. My plan was to teach kids that being prepared requires time and planning and how procrastinating can leave us with too little time to make good decisions. By wearing one hot pink and one sky blue high-top tennis shoe, the students would see an illustration of my message.

"Of course, those shoes wouldn't match anything, even if you had two of the same color. Whoever heard of those colors for shoes? Don't know why you bought them," my mother continued.

"Oh, Shirley, let it go," Dad said, without turning away from the TV screen. "If she wants to go out of the house looking like nobody loves her ... that's her."

Great, now my dad had implemented the guilt strategy usually reserved as a last ditch effort by most parents.

"Mom, I'm taking a spare pair of shoes to change into. See, these match." I held up the alternates. She looked relieved, as though it had just been proven that I really wasn't a two-headed monster living in the shell of my former self.

"I want to make a point with 13-year-olds. And you know how important appearance is to them. It's just part of my plan to get their attention." That did it. My mother was happy again. She even put her cigarettes back in her purse. She checked on the biscuits in the oven and then did something that would have driven me to smoke, if I smoked at all, that is. She joined my father in his television viewing trance. The two of them sitting at the kitchen table, swaying, flinching and celebrating at the same highlights. Yikes! So that's what more than three decades of marriage looks like. And she's worried about my shoes!

* * * * *

That morning with my parents shows that sometimes even a well-thought-out plan can seem to make no sense. I had a reason for wearing shoes that clashed with my outfit, but to an observer like my mom, my plan was ill-conceived or, at best, confusing.

That's how God's plan for our lives may seem to us. Things happen and seem to make no sense. Good and bad things leave us scratching our heads, frustrated like my mom was that day. But in the end there was a certain and purposeful plan involving my shoes, she just needed to see it revealed.

Our part in learning God's plan for us is simple in theory, but often difficult for many people to execute. To begin to understand His plan for us, we need to be open to receiving His love and guidance. For a lot of people, that's much easier said than done. This has to do with our willingness to be molded by God. If we think of ourselves as clay and God as the potter, just like an artist, He fashions us to his liking. And just like a good lump of clay, we must stay malleable and ready.

So the first step in learning His plan for you is to open your heart and mind to any and all possibilities. Then, with that established, pray for God to show you the meaning or purpose of events in your life. Pray that the plan be revealed through a teacher or an opportunity. And you must pray without any expectation. In other words, don't tell God what you hope is His plan. First, give Him some time to show you His way. This will take patience.

* * * * *

If you're not patient and you want to take more immediate steps to learn God's plan for your life, there is something you can do. In Chapter 6, "Sow Ten Seeds for Success," you read about the gifts God gives us. His plan is almost always tied to these gifts. These are not material things. God's gifts are those skills or talents we seem to have naturally. Figure out what your key gift is, and you may find that life somehow is either pulling you in that direction, or there's a desire so strong in your heart for that gift that you must use it. That could be a crucial part of His plan for you.

For years, I considered my voice to be a curse. In grade school, my mouth was constantly getting me into trouble. Saying exactly what was on my mind was definitely a hazard. But, as I got older, it became apparent that my ability to clearly express myself was not only an advantage but a necessity in striving for success in the incredibly competitive field of TV journalism. Everyone in that business is a talker.

What is your gift? If you answered that you don't have one, or you're not sure, let's find your gift. Take out a piece of paper and something to write with. Make a list of things that you're good at. Some of you may have a more impressive list than others at first glance. For instance, one person may write down the gift of being a classic pianist. Someone else may be good at getting plants to grow. No one gift is any more special than another. God's blessings are individual, and the scope of their potential has nothing to do with how people would judge their importance.

Maybe your gift is as simple as baking delicious cookies. That's how Debbie Fields got started. I interviewed her on a visit with Girl Scouts in Kansas City in April of 1999. Debbie told me when her five daughters were young, she often baked them cookies. Debbie was **gifted** at putting just the right amount of certain ingredients together to make her daughters and anyone else long for more and more cookies. Her gift turned out to be a blessing for her entire family. She told me it took years of hard work and dedication to form the super successful company Mrs. Fields Cookies. But Debbie says she knew her gift was a crucial part of God's plan for her life, and so she pursued it completely. Now, God's plan is leading her to use another of her gifts. Debbie is a dynamic public speaker, motivating people the world over to fight the odds and press on for financial freedom in their lives.

Not everyone's gifts will make him/her a millionaire. However, those skills are the most likely to have divine power behind them.

Once you've written down your list of gifts, shorten that list again to the number one action that you think you execute as well as or better than anyone you know. Also, this must be something that can benefit others. In my case, it was the use of my voice. To date, I use my voice to tell other people's stories on the evening news.

I believe God's plan for my life includes being a responsible journalist. My voice is necessary for that. And His plan involves me using the public notoriety that comes with being on television to reach young people with a message. I use my voice again to teach teenagers the benefits of getting an education and nurturing a positive attitude in everything they do. And I use my voice to talk with other crime victims about being empowered in their situations and not giving up hope for a positive end. That's the lesson I learned from being stalked. My voice is crucial to God's plan for my life.

Identifying your key gift may take longer than a few minutes. It may help to actually do some of the things you're good at and see which one stands out as exceptional, fulfilling and helpful to others. My friend Wendy Wahlstedt is a good example of how having many gifts can mislead you about God's plan for your life.

From an early age, Wendy was fascinated by air travel. She loves airplanes. She's always excelled at tasks such as parking cars, because she has a special understanding of depth and distance. So it was only natural for her to want to be a pilot. And after completing flight school and acquiring her own airplane, it appeared Wendy would someday fly huge jets for a commercial airline. At least, that's what *she* wanted. But for years all Wendy could find were opportunities as a flight instructor involving small planes, not jets. She flew many hours trying to qualify for airline consideration. It just didn't happen. Wendy was a talented pilot, but she would learn that's not her key gift. Wendy's outstanding gift from God is her ability to never give up no matter what the odds. At five feet two inches tall and barely tipping the scales over 110 pounds, Wendy is constantly challenged by men who doubt her skills. And, in return, she amazes them with her will — a good life example for young people to witness. Maybe that's why God had Wendy teaching for so long. When talking with other instructors it was apparent she was instructing some of the youngest flight school students around. Her key gift of determination was being passed on to them.

God's plan for Wendy, it appears, did eventually include her flying big commercial jets. She has finally gotten to that level. But because her path to get there included teaching, young women and men are benefiting. In her spare time, when she's not flying for an airline, she's still teaching young people to fly ... showing them that being a pilot has nothing to do with gender and everything to do with one's will.

* * * * *

As you search for God's plan for your life, you can pray for a revelation which takes patience. Or you can take action by identifying the key gift tied to His plan and pursuing its possibilities to the fullest. Either way, you must be aware that you will never know all of the answers or parts of the plan because it's not a destination. None of us gets to live through pain and struggle and happiness just so we can reach some magical point where it's all perfect and blissful. Discovering your purpose is not the end, it's the beginning.

CHAPTER EIGHT

Breaking News Update: The Stalker's Return

THREAT ASSESSMENT STATISTICS show that the average stalker pursues his victim for 12 years. I can only assume the man who targeted me is average and that I'm only a part of the way into what could be a long period of sporadic contact with him.

And that appears to be the case. It's a felony for him to call or come near me in the state of Missouri. But when the stalker reappeared, I wasn't in Missouri. In the summer of 1997, the man convicted of stalking me for nearly two years was back.

I was at a journalist convention at the North Shore Hilton in Chicago. Running into friends and colleagues at the workshops and dressy dinners was great fun. On the final evening of that five-day trip, I received a disturbing message on the hotel room voice mail. A man's voice spoke slowly and deliberately.

"Hi, there. This is your nemesis from the past. Miss me? Don't worry, I'm not far away. Saw you tonight through the doors of the banquet hall. I lost my ticket and couldn't attend, but I wanted to see how you were dressed. Who was that guy you were talking to? The one with the gold bow tie. Don't tell me. Let me guess. He can't help your career, but you must think he's cute. You're so stupid.

"I can help you now. I work for NBC — at the top. Let's just say I can put you where you want to be, that is, if you're nice to me. I'm staying at a hotel down Michigan Avenue. And obviously I can find you — at least for the next day. And there's nothing they can do about it here in Illinois."

The dial tone finally broke the grip his voice had on my soul. It was after one in the morning, and I was scared to death — again. Just then, the phone rang. It was the hotel operator. She said a security guard was on his way up to my room. She had fielded several calls from a man whom she described as spooky.

She said the man demanded several times to be connected to my room and to be told my room number. He sounded upset because no one answered the phone in my room. The hotel traced the calls the stalker had made to a guest phone on the second floor. When a security guard reached that area, he had vanished. Hotel security suggested I take an earlier flight back to Missouri, leaving the next morning rather than staying for a gospel brunch and other events. The bottom line, in Missouri the law protected me, but in Illinois I was exposed, at least that's what the hotel guard said.

Chicago police were called by the hotel to follow my cab to the outskirts of town heading out to the airport. It was a very sad day for me, partially because the police kept calling me "the victim." Also, because I knew that the hotel guard and the police weren't telling me the whole story about what this guy had said or possibly threatened to do to the hotel operator if she didn't help him. I was simply told it was better that I not know and that I leave quickly. I hated that. I thought I'd overcome people trying to give me a dose of what they thought was better for me than the truth. Defeat, that's what I felt. All of my persistence, the trial, all of it seemed to unravel in a few phone calls that occurred across state lines. And the stalker got what he wanted. But maybe not.

When I returned home to Kansas City, I had another phone message waiting for me. This time it was a woman cop — a 12-year veteran with the Chicago Police Department. A tough voice, with confidence yet sympathy, spoke to my voice mail, "Ms. Faulkner, you were not treated right when you were in our city, and I want to follow up with you. You were given some wrong information. Please call me at area code 312 ...."

When I returned her phone call, the officer explained that my court-ordered protection from the stalker came under interstate laws and I was just as safe in Illinois as I would be anywhere in the United States. She wanted me to know that so I wouldn't fear going on with my life wherever that might lead me. She told me she thought I was brave to have survived such a mentally trying ordeal and she was glad to meet me, even if only by telephone. My feelings of defeat and fear turned once again to empowerment and pride in my persistence. I realized that because of the nature of the crime and the psychology of the criminal, there may exist a threat to me for some time to come. However, I will not let that overshadow my accomplishments or relationships because God's plan is for me to be stronger than that. I will live according to that plan and no one else's ... never losing faith along the way.

WHAT EVERY STALKING VICTIM SHOULD KNOW

No one will be a better advocate for you than you!

1. Find out what your city/county/state laws say about stalking.

2. Find out which unit at your local police department deals with stalking complaints. Inform them of your situation.

3. If you know the identity of the stalker, go to court to petition for a restraining order or papers of protection to keep him/her away from you, your home and your job.

4. Take a self-defense course that teaches the basics of personal safety. This will help you build self-esteem and confidence.

5. If you choose to carry mace, pepper spray or purchase a gun, learn to use it properly. And be aware these weapons can be turned and used against you.

6. Confide in someone you trust, so that another person is familiar with your situation. Be careful talking about it in public places, because you never know who the stalker may befriend to get near you.

7. Avoid becoming a target. Use the buddy system. Don't walk in dark parking lots or areas at night alone.

8. Install a telephone caller identification device on your home phone.

9. Have at least one telephone in your home that needs no electricity to work. That way if the power to your home goes out, you can still use your phone.

10. Help police/prosecutors do their job. Build a case against your stalker. Keep a log of incidents complete with dates and times. Save voice mail messages that contain threats.

11. Don't be embarrassed or intimidated to call 911.

12. Don't stop living your life. Find ways to have fun and to relax. If you're all stressed out and allowing your mind to only focus on the stalker, you lose.